May 1, 2012

Sherry

I wanted to take time to tell you how much I have enjoyed coming to know you. You are one of the sweetest most loving people I have ever met. At times I was very sad that my time here was temporary as it kept me from knowing you better, knowing I had to leave. Just so you know, all my flirting was sincere and my backing off was because I like you more than I wanted to be selfish. I so appreciate your caring for me, making me feel special and becoming special to me.

Thank you so much for learning about me, liking me and making me feel special to you.

Yours always...

Friends First

Does that mean we go Dutch or just no Sex???

By

Jeremiah J. Jordan

A View of Adult Dating and Relationships.

AuthorHouse™
1663 Liberty Drive
Bloomington, IN 47403
www.authorhouse.com
Phone: 1-800-839-8640

© 2012 by Jeremiah J. Jordan. All rights reserved.

No part of this book may be reproduced, stored in a retrieval system, or transmitted by any means without the written permission of the author.

Published by AuthorHouse   02/28/2012

ISBN: 978-1-4685-5522-6 (sc)
ISBN: 978-1-4685-5521-9 (hc)
ISBN: 978-1-4685-5520-2 (e)

Library of Congress Control Number: 2012903307

Any people depicted in stock imagery provided by Thinkstock are models, and such images are being used for illustrative purposes only.
Certain stock imagery © Thinkstock.

This book is printed on acid-free paper.

Because of the dynamic nature of the Internet, any web addresses or links contained in this book may have changed since publication and may no longer be valid. The views expressed in this work are solely those of the author and do not necessarily reflect the views of the publisher, and the publisher hereby disclaims any responsibility for them.

Contents

Acknowledgements vii

Forward xi

Chapter 1   The Promise 1

Chapter 2   The Problem 7

Chapter 3   Communication 29

Chapter 4   Grown Up Relationships 59

Chapter 5   The Scale 79

Chapter 6   Hope? 105

Acknowledgements

I would like to ardently thank Sydney Clark for her tireless efforts to turn my words and thoughts from a sow's ear to at least a near-silk purse. Her ability to embrace the subject matter, both from my perspective as well as with an objective eye, was paramount to its saying what I had hoped it would. Thank you so very much.

To my sons . . . I can never say I love you often enough nor can I find ways to show you that will even closely resemble to you how deeply I feel for you. We cannot always live our lives as we should. We can always stand steadfastly beside those we love and wish for them the best of what may come. I am happy beyond words that, with you both, The Dream is still alive and well. With the patience of my wonderful daughters-in-law, neither of you will have need for this book.

To Rhoda, Jean, and Dianna. One gave me life, one gave me direction and one gave me hope.

To all those I have loved,

Thank you.

*It is oddly embarrassing when we finally realize
what a truly momentous life we are fortunate to have lived.*

Jeremiah J. Jordan, 2011

Forward

I have heard for years about all the things wrong with men. Most often I have heard it from women, and I continue to listen to women's complaints regarding men. I remember it being said that men are "chauvinist pigs," that they should evolve, and that men are only after one thing. I have been told that men shouldn't be shallow, that they should see a woman for the person she really is, not how she looks. It has been said, over and over, that men shouldn't treat women as objects. To all that, and more . . .
I agree.

Men are slime. Men are shallow. Men are interested in only one thing when they date. Men lie and pretend and say anything to further their way to the desired outcome. When it comes to relationships with women, men are generally untrustworthy, unfaithful, and worst of all, willing to trade in a woman for a newer model. Did I miss anything?

Oh yes, men have a similar depth of negative feelings about women. But that is another story.

While listening to hundreds of conversations over the past twenty years with women, as well as from listening to men when women weren't around, I have come to appreciate the differences between men and women and the expectations and frustrations of both as they try to find relationships that can work. I believe both are right and both are wrong. Frustration between the sexes is a product of our collective biology as well as our long-fought history. We try to fit our personal journey of relationship discovery into an ever-changing culture, often with considerable regret for our effort. Our technology is giving us options for communication which we couldn't imagine just a few years ago. Often the human in us can't keep up or appreciate the speed of the many changes to our lives and how it will affect aspects of our pursuit of a relationship. What was on the cutting edge two years ago is now mild, passé and has changed without pause.

This gives us more choices as well as more opportunities to succeed and fail. All things come to us as a double edge sword. That is the frustrating balance upon which the universe depends.

A part of the delicate balance in our universe is the desire for humans to couple. Throughout the human condition that desire has continued to direct much of our thoughts and behaviors, from the time we wandered, hunted and gathered to survive to today's first-meet dates at Starbucks. As difficult as it is, we are constantly drawn back to dating, often against our will and in conflict with our fear; we can't help but ponder the big "what if." If we didn't, dating sites would not be as popular. We still date, still want to be with someone, and still want to be liked. We still make the same mistakes, still deal with the same feelings that have beset our species since first we had conscious thought.

Remember back when you were in school and how strange boys were. They started to notice the girl who had been sitting next to them for years. All of a sudden, when she was near, his palms began to sweat, he couldn't talk right anymore. She smelled so good to him and he couldn't stop thinking about her. He had known her for years and there was no surprise about who she was, or where she came from. There was no mystery about what she believed, what she liked and didn't like. It was truly *Friends First*.

Except they weren't real friends. Nothing much was shared; usually teasing proved to be the means of communication at that point in time. If they started dating, the couple was connected at the hip. She thought it was significant when a boy told her his dreams of the future. It was romantic and joyous to share a grown up dream. The girl could see more in the boy than truly was there because she didn't have the life experience to know the difference. The realities of life had not yet set in.

Grown up girls—women—like the idea of being "connected at the hip." The adolescent memory of it is comforting. It's like being "friends" but again, not *real* friends. Not like with female friends. Depending on which side of sexual behavior you find yourself, the idea of being connected at the hip changes significantly. Once sex is introduced, the buddy is gone; the "friend" is lost in the lust of youth

For adolescent males, sex with a female is the goal. It is viewed as a prize. It becomes nearly all consuming for a time during adolescence. Boys are not really sure why it is, they are just driven to it. It is when males begin to struggle with the temptation to say anything to reach the goal and come to realize there are several ways to succeed. This is not new behavior for males and it has been constant since we began as a species. This is also when men realize, if they haven't already, the race for female favor isn't fair, or at least not on a level playing field. Looks, talent, and money all affect the level of success a young man has in gaining female favor. Whether those differences are real or perceived, the lessons learned are carried into adulthood and they greatly affect future behavior. The residual unconscious attachment to the original learning echoes in the mind during the adult dating process for both men and women.

Puberty: Gotta Love It

Girls are taught a very different view of sexuality than boys. The official word is not intended to be different but there is a difference because, between boys and girls, only one can give birth. This is why we still view girls differently than boys socially, culturally, and sexually and consistently reinforce that through our media, social interactions, and parenting. The messages are confusing primarily because of the intense attempt to protect girls from boys and, therefore, pregnancy. That makes a lot of sense if we try to understand the idea of why a woman would feel that becoming Friends First is safer. Becoming Friends First would seem to provide some time for learning if she wants to keep the man and, hopefully, if he is worth keeping. All of this could be accomplished before the man achieves his primary goal and decides if he is staying or leaving.

I believe women deserve better from men. I am just not convinced men can deliver.

When looking at the Relationship section of your local big-box bookstore, it often seems that most books written about male/female dating and relationships discuss the issue from a female perspective. There appears to be precious little "manly" material on the same subject matter cluttering the shelves. More often than not, popular titles seem to indicate ways to manage the male in a relationship while he "grows up." Or, from a somewhat less sensitive perspective, female writers try to set some standards for men to follow so that women can be assured of not getting hurt, despite the woman's own behavior.

There seems to be a line of thought that men can be coaxed from the primordial ooze and be more than they are. Or more than they think they are. Maybe that thought pattern works along the premise that men can be forced to evolve into caring, feeling beings that are still filled with testosterone, hence becoming "real men." That whole sentence confused me when I wrote it, and it still does. For some reason when I think of women trying to do this it reminds me of the desire to have one's cake and eat it too. For those of you who have attempted this, how is it working for you? I think all those books have killed a lot of trees and delayed potential happiness for many women.

Contrary to the natural inclination of the male of the species, there seems to be an underlying belief that men's genetic proclivities can be overlooked and their behavior can be programmed. In simple terms, instead of men dating for sex, they date for a woman's personality, for their mind, for their good qualities, kindness and work ethic. A woman's physical appearance would have no influence on the decision. Maybe we have found some equality between the genders which has allowed for a more sensitive man to exist, a man who is able to go beyond their lustful ways and embrace a more holistic woman.

Yeah like that's really going to happen. So ladies . . . how's that working out for you?

The basics between men and woman have not changed since we first walked the earth. Our instincts are intact and functioning. We cannot help who we are attracted to, who we like or especially who we love. We can't control how we get there or how long we remain. Our species procreates and survives on those instincts. As we became civilized, a social order developed with rules about females, sex, and how the differences between men and women are to be treated. Law took on a formalization of the concept that a woman's body was her own and no one had the right to violate it without consequence. While this has been customary in many cultures for centuries, the most prevalent view was to place all weight of an indiscretion on the women. It happened because of her and the consequences would fall to her. In the patriarchal cultures which proceeded the current era, women were treated as possessions, passed from father to husband without having sexual relations. A great value was placed upon virginity. This value came from the female's lack of carnal knowledge. If you don't know, you have nothing to compare. No reason to question that life, or love, could be better elsewhere. It also created considerable control for the men and kept women as possessions. The rules of marriage were written by men, fathers, and husbands of the time, ensuring a woman could not refuse her husband's sexual demands. I truly believe that this was done as a result of the recognition of the irresistible pull a woman has on a man in a sexual way. The difference in how men and woman perceive sex and relationships in this ownership concept created a vast amount of confusion. This book will look at many of the subsequent and lingering dilemmas and, while not attempting to resolve any of them, will perhaps allow for some reflection and perspective.

None of the statements, generalizations, or assertions in this book have been shown to be absolute in any empirical analysis. Any information here is anecdotal. That being said, if any truths are reflected upon, either by design or accidentally, the author will feel good about it, albeit a little surprised.

While the information in this book is anecdotal, it bears some significance if only by the nods, laughing, and humorous generalizations which come out of conversations about dating and relationships. The comments and statements made in this book, which seem to be statements of fact, are intended to be generalizations. These generalizations, in a statistical sense, would represent seven out of ten or seventy percent of the group mentioned. In other words, all generalizations used in the book are without research to confirm validity. This book is intended to be humorous at the expense of both genders and perhaps to show why we are disappointed when our desires don't pan out. If we refuse to see what is obvious it is our own fault and, like it or not, we deserve the consequences.

As mentioned before but worth repeating, references to all men or all women is intended to be a generalization which applies to only about seventy percent of either population. There are exceptions and, it is accepted that everyone who reads this book knows someone who is different in one way or another. While it's nice to know that this unique situation exists, my dad used to tell me "*The race doesn't always go to the stronger, faster man . . . but that is the way to bet.*" We use generalities for a reason because they hold truths.

This book attempts to speak to the confusion in communication between men and women. Hopefully, it can shed some light on what we, both men and women, want and how poor we are at expressing it and therefore getting it. It is my hope that those reading this book will look at their own dating situation and be able to smile and perhaps be more understanding of the process. We all want happiness. We all want to be loved. Understanding, even humorous understanding, is a good thing.

Chapter 1

The Promise

A woman wants a friend with whom she falls in love and he becomes a great lover.

A man wants a great lover with whom he falls in love and she becomes a friend.

Jeremiah J. Jordan, 2011

It began as a promise from my mother. Never from my father or any man had I known. It was repeated by the women in my mother's life—the first females in my young life. It was pounded into me from stories, rumors, and chats with friends. From older kids I received a lot of partially true information about how grown-up boys and girls acted together and what things *might* be like, at night, in the dark. It was all a great mystery in the mind of a curious young boy.

Mom was quite clear to me at a very early age. When I had any questions about marriage, about relationships, about boys and girls, she would always respond to me with "*Somewhere, out there, is 'The One'—your true love—and you will find her*". This was a very simple, yet intriguing, concept for a child to begin to comprehend. Out in the huge world was one person made especially for me, a perfect fit, and my true love. So I accepted that promise and began looking for "The One." When I was about twelve-years-old, I remember asking my mother a very important question: "*What if she lives in China?*" Her response was simple, pragmatic: "*Somehow you will find a way to meet and be together.*" When I was twelve-years-old, that was a believable answer. As I got older and realized how far away China really was, it became less believable.

All the fairy tales I had been reading as a child told me the same thing. Movies and TV shows drove home the concept of that seemingly elusive being. Disney was heavily invested in "happily ever-after." On the radio, love songs reinforced the illusion of "The One"—a marketing strategy that surely played to the fragile emotions of the love-sated teenage population, dying from isolation and loneliness as they begrudgingly accepted their despair at not having "The One" that surely was meant for them. There were the lucky ones, though, and all I had to do was look around at those who had found their "One" and breathe a sigh of relief, knowing that somewhere, out there, was my "One."

The Promise was powerful. It was calming and reassuring to know out there in that giant, confusing and frightening world that somewhere was a perfect fit made just for me. It made adolescent rejection easier to swallow because "The One" was out there. I just had to be patient and endure. It made "puppy love" and being "not enough" and girls wanting to be "friends" somewhat more bearable. If I hadn't known about "The One,"

I would have felt very miserable when the cute girl silently exploded with laughter when I asked her to dance. Suddenly, I was the obvious topic of girl-talk as I retreated, head down, broken, back across the dance floor after this painful rejection. But I had The Promise.

Friends Only, Please . . .

The Promise began to be less helpful when the girl I had a huge crush on would say, "*You're really great, but I think of you **only** as a friend.*" Even then I recognized friendship with a female to be a negative relationship. It was full of doing stuff for her, at her beck and call, ignoring my wants and needs, all the while watching her with other boys. She would smile and tell me how wonderful it was to have me around to depend upon. That now-and-again hug I received from her actually meant less to her than the occasional hug she gave to the uncle she barely knew and rarely saw. What a demoralizing experience this was; that, along with the knowledge that she was steaming the windows with boys who would never care for her as I did. Oh, Adolescence! How I don't miss thee.

There was, of course, the more popular and totally destroying line, *"I only want to be friends."* OUCH! Why didn't she just hit me with a heavy, sharp object and put me out of my misery? Those words still echo in my ears. I can tell you every time they were spoken, by whom and where. Sometimes I remember the music that was playing, and it's usually with the memory of the crushing blow that had just landed. There are times I pass a woman and her perfume takes me back to that time, that moment, that painful experience as if I am still there. Joy comes and goes but grief, humiliation, personal injury from another, even if unintentional, lasts forever. Perhaps in some cases it would have been easier if it had been intentional. At least you would have registered on her radar.

I think it was during that time when I began to hate the word "friend." Most guys I know hate the word and always have. Often we use the expression "friend" in the same way we use the shallow expression, *"How are you?"* with strangers. We are programmed to express sentiment via habit and custom, not always from the heart. Unlike Greek, with its categorized expressions for the word *love*, the English language does not possess a word that fits between "friend" and "lover."

It seems that for girls and women, "friend" has come to mean something like no risk, harmless, or no physical connection. That is how it played out as teenagers and how it seems to play out as grown-ups. The true significance of a woman's view of "friends" is telling in the way they assure a third party—usually a boyfriend or husband—of someone's lack of significance, and that the male acquaintance or co-worker is benign to her. *"Oh, we're just friends."* That wasn't lost on me at fifteen and it isn't lost on me now. So, from my point of view, knowing how a person interprets the word they are saying is what it means to them. If being a woman's "friend" results in a neutral relationship, what is the point? "Friend" is not a word that describes anything a man wants to be with a woman. And, all these years later, women are still throwing the "friend" word around like it's a good thing. Duhhhhh, NO! That doesn't mean we can't *be* friends, or won't be a friend. It just means that isn't what we *want* to be. We often want to be more, sometimes we want to be less, and we never, ever want to be *only*.

Top Phrases Men Hate from Women
(Have You Used Any?)

- I just want to be friends. ("*You will emotionally support me but I will get my sex elsewhere.*") see the movie—*The Last American Virgin*

- I think of you as a friend. ("*I think of you as gay or a eunuch or ugly . . .*" or worse yet . . . *not enough.*)

- I don't want sex to mess up our friendship. (What if I don't want friendship to mess up our sex?) And, since it's the woman's choice about sex—unless you want to go to prison—men have to go along with it—and hope she'll change her mind.

- I don't want to lose your friendship . . . (see above)

- I still want to be friends. (You might as well look us in the eye and say *"You're not enough"* . . . or just shoot us.)

In a man's own mind, not being enough is like not being. It is how to cut a man to the core of his being. Women so often throw it around passively with no regard for the men they aim it at because they don't seem to understand how damaging this can be. I know men are no angels and often get what they deserve, but in a world of promise for "The One," how do we communicate so badly about something so important?

The Promise echoes in the thoughts of both men and women. For women, The Promise represents the idea that if a man isn't "The One," then they can always be friends. For men, The Promise almost becomes a contradiction in terms. Those feelings of friendship verses lover/sexual partner are so confusing to guys. Since we don't date to create a friendship, but rather a means to the end goal of sexual encounter and ultimately a permanent lover, it becomes a real struggle to believe in The Promise. It seems to be a true dichotomy and once we lose faith in what our female nurturers *promised* us, our perspective changes toward dating.

It is important to understand that men and women are not consciously conspiring against each other. Instead, the promise given to all of us was a means of softening the emotional blow of adolescence and growing up in an often not-so-loving world. The Promise influenced our thinking and expectations so that we could control our behavior toward one another and reduce promiscuity, therefore controlling the gene pool to a greater or lesser extent. The honeybee/honeysuckle, yin/yang of life is effectively controlled by The Promise. It's a sweet dream and something in which we all want to believe. Like romantic comedy, happy endings, and fairy tales, we desperately want "The One" to be out there for us. We want to be loved, perhaps more than we want to love in return. As grown-ups, we have been let down, hurt, and often emotionally damaged beyond repair. But, always, there is the expectation that The Promise gives us hope and a way to come back and try—again and again.

Chapter 2

The Problem

With tears in her eyes, her heart full and her emotions overflowing, in that brief moment of horror she labeled me the thing I was most fearful of being . . . a friend.

Jeremiah J. Jordan, 2011

Men choose a woman hoping she will not change. Women choose a man hoping he will

Anonymous

This book was not intentionally started as a referendum on friends. It was intended to be a new look at adult dating and relationships. "Friend" is such a recurring issue between men and women and the word causes much confusion, frustration, and contempt because it is so completely misunderstood by and between the sexes. With this in mind, I feel the need to address the concept of "friend" in adult dating and relationships since it doesn't seem to be avoidable. The word "friend' isn't the problem but rather confusion about the word, how we came to be confused about it, and how the word is perceived by men and women. That is The Problem.

For men and women, the word *friend* can have different meanings and this difference in meanings, as it pertains to the sexes, can have a polarizing effect upon communication between the two. The subtle nuances of the word can play havoc with individual expectations in a relationship. It can play tricks with our collective memories, as well. When we were children, adolescents, and young adults, *friend* meant something entirely different. As full grown adults, complete with historical relationships, this playful little word can take on a life of its own. Rarely does one word provoke so many different ideas, feelings, and opinions.

The English language is excellent in communicating technical material. It is extremely efficient with academic material and general communication between colleagues. English does a wonderful job of passing non-emotional communication. When feelings are involved, English is not only inadequate, it totally sucks. The English language performs an excellent butcher-job on "feeling" words. Take, for instance, the word *love*. We "love" ice cream. We "love" our best buddy. We "love" a certain movie. We "love" art (or music, sports, epicurean delights, etc.) We have the "love" of God. We make "love." We have the "love" of our life. I (insert heart icon) my wife/husband/significant other/dog/cat . . . you name it. One word, different feelings and meanings. Contrast with the Greek: *agape* (God love); *Eros* (sensual/sexual love); *philia* (brotherly/friend love); *storge* (affectionate love). Four words, multiple feelings and meanings.

The word "friend" also can mean something different to each individual and in different circumstances. I have a "best friend." A fourteen-year-old girl has a "best friend forever" (BFF in text language). You might invite your "friends" over for dinner next Friday. He and his "buddies" (friends) watch the game every Saturday. Harry and Sally are "just friends." Contrast this with how divided men and women are by their nature and how very differently they use the word "friend" and what it means in their lives. Communication makes a difference and we often aren't communicating the subtle differences in "friendship" with each other. Oftentimes we throw out the word "friend" because it catches so many things we may feel, or don't want to express. It's much easier to say, *"I want to be friends"* than what you really mean: *"I find you totally unattractive and wouldn't allow you to put your mouth on me even if I needed CPR."*

"Friend" is often used in place of acquaintance. "Friend" is often used to imply less or more feeling. *"He is only a friend"* or *"I count them as one of my closest, dearest friends."* The idea in and of itself that the word "friend" can be used either to imply things 180° apart in meaning should tell us something significant about ourselves, others, and the use of the word "friend." When we use it, we generally aren't saying what we really want to say. So, how can we expect someone to know what we mean?

A Greeting Card Moment

There is an old internet joke that has floated around for years and I am sure was around in some form long before that. *There are a hundred ways to tell a woman you care about her: flowers, gifts, dinner, candy, a surprise phone call just to see how she is doing. A card or just saying she is appreciated tells a woman I CARE FOR YOU.* For men it's a little different: *To tell a man you care, come naked—bring beer.* I have also heard it said *come naked—bring food.* The message is quite clear and too true if we look at many of the problems between men and women trying to have a relationship. Perhaps that is why we find it more than humorous. I don't know who said it first or where I heard it and I do laugh about it with the rest of you. It also makes me a little sad because it clearly defines our incredible differences in how we perceive one another. Our needs, wants, and happiness have been broken down into a cliché. Yet, the truth in the joke is staggering in how it affects our behavior, expectations, and happiness. When we carefully look at that difference between us, it underlies how we view relationship development.

We communicate in a way we want others to communicate to us. We compliment to receive compliments, we do things for others that we want them to do for us. I have often pointed to greeting cards, flowers, gifts, and phone calls for no reason as the benchmarks of what women feel are signs of romance and caring. Women communicate with one another using these methods of sharing care. If we look at how men communicate, we can see that the process is very different. If it were left up to men, if there were no perceived benefit to them for using those tangible poofs of care, greeting card makers and florists would go bankrupt in about thirty days. Were it not for women, either giving to one another or being received from a man trying to gain favor, they would be used hardly at all. That men use them, even with grudging reluctance, is because women love these signs of affection and want to receive them. Men respond to reinforcement, so if flowers, candy, or cards gain favor, they do it more and more as a means to an end. It doesn't matter that the concept or feelings involved totally escapes them.

DNA Rocks Our World

Romance novels, romantic comedies and, yes, fairy tales ("they lived happily ever-after") give us the impression that there is "The One" out there who will complete us. Are any of them truly reflective of real relationships or the people in them? While this fits so well with "The Promise" we all learned and believed in, does it bear itself out? Perhaps there is, out there, "The One." How do we find that person? Men and women are programmed with a search engine for the survival of our species. Our mating mechanisms are coded into our DNA. This has a profound impact upon how we search. This search method is probably the defining difference between men and women. While each sex's search engine is identical in properties and both lead to the same destination, the journey is what all the fuss is about. They are as different as East and West, as far apart as Siberia from Oklahoma. So, yes, men and women really do see the world differently. If we accept the idea that all of us are looking for "The One," why is the process so hard?

It would be very easy to think that the difference lies completely in our biological imprint. Our DNA drives us in directions we are just beginning to understand. Back in hunter-gatherer days, for *homo sapiens*, women were the caregivers. They needed support during pregnancy and until the time that children were old enough to fend for themselves. Men were an integral part of the relationship because, as well as providing the seed to procreate, they would provide food, shelter, and security for the female while she was pregnant and the children were young.

It was a symbiotic relationship held together by procreation and survival. Males were driven to breed, as were females, and each searched for an appropriate partner with which to perpetuate the species as well as nurture and protect. Both needed to make appropriate choices based on health and prowess. Somewhere along the line, love and affection must have entered into the mix. And, with the male's biological urge to mate and the female's need to nurture, it seems likely that, over millennia, love and affection for one another began to supplant communal needs.

The difference lies in the male's need for sex at any opportunity (to spread genetics in a wide swath) that is later (with the selection of a "steady" mate) accompanied with the secure feelings found in love and affection. For women, the eternal nurturers and caregivers, love and affection *first* may have offered a change to achieve an acceptable comfort level with a potential mate *before* pregnancy, and the possibility of good (or poor) genetics taking place, i.e., the begetting of strong, healthy, offspring. Why take a chance on a mate that may not be strong enough to make it through hard times when, with a little patience, one could wait until a stronger male proved his worth by bringing home the mastodon while "proving" himself in the field. For males, the opposite may be quite obvious: why give up a golden opportunity to spread genetics before a stronger male gathered up the goodies? No point in wasting time on nurturing (the realm of the female) when a saber-tooth may take you out tomorrow. Besides, who wants to hang around camp waiting to starve when dinner-on-the-hoof roamed the land, waiting to be harvested? A woman needed to make good choices concerning a breeding partner and a man, well, a man just needs. Men, then as now, no matter what the age, are driven to breed even if they no longer have the capacity or plumbing.

Stipulations

Nonetheless, today's woman says it differently: *"Men are always thinking with the wrong head." "Sex first, then friendship? I don't think so." "Men need to treat women like they care about them." "He only thinks of me as a sex object." "I just want him to listen to me, care about me, and understand me." "I need him to become one with me in soul and spirit. You know, my soul-mate." "If only he cared about the inner me."* These aren't selfish requests but rather a reflection of the need to nurture and cultivate a relationship, even though the biological mechanisms may have shut down. In other words, desire originates in the brain.

Additional "requests" show up on dating sites:

WANTED: *Mature, sophisticated, fun loving, nurturing male over 6' tall who loves the outdoors, is physically fit, financially stable and, most importantly, can enjoy the things I want to do.*

HIDDEN AGENDA: *Gay guy who obviously won't touch me but will satisfy my need to be with a man from time to time, if only for appearance sake.*

Please, ladies . . . apparently you want your cake and prefer to pack on the calories by eating it, too.

Every time a condition is added, statistically, the number of people who can meet the requirement gets smaller. By qualifying potential partners, women often cut themselves out of the playing field. Of course, no one, woman or man, should settle for someone who is not up to basic requirements (i.e., safe from various kinds of abuse, a lack of physical attraction, intellectual differences, etc.); however, by qualifying beyond what is reasonable, the statistical gene pool (or dating pool) decreases exponentially. Ladies, maybe you should consider going back to basics.

Men have their qualifiers, too. They may *ask* for a woman who is smart, pretty, clever, sexy (looking), dresses well, is independent, etc., but what they really want is basic stuff: a good (or at least a decent) cook, is attractive (i.e., knows how to dress, doesn't need a lot of make-up, gets her hair done regularly), doesn't nag or complain, picks up after him, and . . . loves sex . . . preferably a lot. Men don't state these qualifications that much, but it's often true. Lessening the extraneous requirements keeps the number of options open for eligible men.

Cost vs. Benefit Analysis

I hear a lot from women about "I don't want to settle" or "I settled before. I won't again." While I admire the goal, I think we should discuss the impact of that line of reasoning. There are absolutes we must have. Not to be hurt, not to be used, likeable, to have a basic attraction for someone. Beyond that, you're adding options. We dig in our heels and say we aren't going to settle for less than what we want. What if I want Jennifer Anniston? I guess I'm kind of out of luck. Punishing ourselves for choosing wrong before is no guarantee of being right the next time.

Think of it this way:

I can afford a car that costs X amount of dollars but I want a car that costs twice as much.
Do I . . .

A: Refuse to get a car until I can have what I want so I am not settling for less, or

B: Get the best vehicle I can with the resources I have on hand? or

C: Incessantly whine that the car I want should be different?

While people are not cars and, of course, are much more complex, I have seen person after person throw a good relationship away because they refused to settle. The settling existed only in their mind. No matter that they are stubborn and unrealistic and refuse to give ground. People, both men and women, tend to make decisions based on what their last relationship *wasn't* or the price they paid for it. So, they get to refuse to settle. Often, they refuse to settle . . . alone. For a long time . . . a very, very, long time. Once your marketability drops, so do your chances of finding a partner. And, age does matter.

Age Matters a Lot

Why does age matter? In part, because men are sexually driven at any age and, likewise, women outnumber their male counterparts every year. If you apply that to available men, eliminate gay, unstable, or married men playing the field, the discrepancy of available men to women is huge. Over the age of fifty the situation is mind-numbing. And at fifty, a man feels very comfortable dating a thirty-five-year-old and often has the resources to do it. Not that any women are into "resource-driven" dating. That makes the male dating pool significantly larger. Also, men have fewer requirements to date and to see if they want a relationship.

If you sort out the gay men (both in and out of the closet), the obviously physically/mentally deficient, guys who are forty-plus and who "just can't commit," widowers who can't get over their dead wives, and the ones who got hurt when they were twenty and just can't pull out of it, there isn't much out there. Oh, and let's not forget the married ones that play the field . . . not a good choice. There are limited options and qualifiers, while intended to weed out the riff-raff, often drives us towards "I won't settle" cliff. This is why women must truly believe in the promise of "The One," because that is the only way, numerically, with all the qualifiers, they can hope to find a partner. If "The One" is a myth . . . Houston (read women) we have a problem.

Historical Fiction

Men often have trouble getting close to women—not that they don't want to, but because sometimes red flags come up. Having a history means we lug around baggage. It can get in the way. For instance, I listened to an acquaintance tell me how his ex-wife used to measure his level of love and commitment by how often he cleaned the downstairs bathroom without being asked. Once he achieved the frequency requirement, he was then measured by its cleanliness based upon her standards, which seemed to change frequently. Then, once the cleanliness and frequency standards were achieved, he was measured by his attitude toward the task. Are you seeing a pattern here? The ever-moving finish line that women—and this is a generalization—seem to be born with makes true commitment difficult because the man doesn't know where it will end. Women seem to find a situation and immediately begin planning for its upgrade. Men like to know beforehand what they are getting and that it won't change. However, women also like to know what they are getting into and very often men have disappointed them. We need to come up with a way to avoid that. Perhaps better communication about what we want and need would be a start.

Friends for Men

Defining friendship for men is difficult unless you're a man. I have often told people you can see a lot in the differences between men and women at the mall food court. Observe a table of women and a table of men. The women are sharing experiences, living each other's feelings and expressing care and concern while enjoying the moment and actually feeling what the other feels. One can hear a great deal of *Oooohhhs!* and *Ahhhhhs!* and *"that is so sweet."* Women seem to live vicariously through each other. Additionally, one will probably hear a great deal of gossip (until the object of the collective group's scorn walks into the feeding frenzy), price comparisons (who was the better bargain hunter), commiseration about the "problem with men" and, last but not least, the collective description by compare and contrast of the birth experience. When children are in attendance (and they usually are), all the women involved serve as caretakers *regardless of the relationship to the children present.* This is probably not unlike the tribal experience where the women in the village work together, laugh and cry together, care for children together, cook and eat together. The bonding of women comes from ancient experience.

The men's table, on the other hand, is boisterous if not vile and disgusting, with each male repeatedly bashing the other. While there is usually a pecking order to activities, all harass one another. Any weakness is immediately pointed out and jeered—and always to the extreme. To men, a friend is someone who always points out the other's mistakes, competes with him constantly, and embarrasses him incessantly. He's a guy with whom you would never share a weakness or feelings because they will be used against you at a later date. Despite this seemingly aggressive behavior, it is important to note that a guy's friends will do anything for him and him for them—then tease each other about having to save their collective butts. Perhaps all of this pointed behavior stems from the days when men had to hunt together for survival and success and, if anyone was weak in the process, he must be weeded out for the survival of the group. Men view other men as competition, so competitiveness is more than likely an issue as well. Even "friends" are seen as competition. Men compete with other men for the prevailing resources at hand (women, food, money, jobs, etc.) and, in ancient times, when resources were scarce, it would have most certainly been hunting party vs. hunting party . . . and may the fastest and sharpest spear win. Besides that, if "he" wins (the greater resource) then "he" may take "my" woman (breeding partner). So, even though the bonds created by men are much different than the bonding that occurs among women, men come by it as naturally as women do, but for different reasons.

Often, it's not about *keeping* something, it's about *getting* something. Women, jobs, cars, and toys are all about "getting." Once you *get it*, well, you have proven you can, so on to the next thing. It's much like adolescent behavior but also very male in scope. *He who dies with the most stuff wins.* It doesn't seem very friendly, but it's okay in the male world. A man will fight another man over a woman, a drink, a place in line, or a piece of pizza, and yet be willing to die for his brother (real friend). For most men, *friend* is a bad word. It's confusing and doesn't really describe that connection we have with our best male friends. Men have many acquaintances. These are people they know and hang out with, do things with, but are not really friends as a man feels it. Some they like a lot. They can spend a great deal of time with both men and women and yet can bond with a couple of real friends they have had since they were young men.

Friendship is a strange and complex relationship among men and is usually created through some difficulty or challenge. It is easy to see the bonds between men who work dangerous jobs. This may have begun during military service or competitive athletics. Jobs like firefighting, law enforcement, logging, mining, and heavy industry all bring danger and the sharing of fear. These jobs have long bonded men into friends and these bonds have come to define the expectation of a level of trust and confidence in one another, or lack thereof. Women have made some inroads towards customarily male jobs and have had some success in developing the types of friendships with men that men have in the past kept only between each other. That barrier was just one of many issues confronted by women during the great role changes we have undergone as they have entered into some primarily male dominated careers.

Men—can't live with them, can't kill them!

For men, it is all interconnected: how we make friends, how we develop relationships, how we search for a partner, and how we communicate. This bonding between men isn't a learned behavior, it's bred into them. That means of connection or friendship is unique to men. We don't generally feel that type of connection for women. It will usually occur only through facing a shared risk or adversity. That is why it is so annoying to hear someone tell us *"you don't have to be that way."* When someone tells us we need to be different, they are making an assertion that our core being is flawed and not right. In a world where we should work to accept and be understanding of others, men are asked to go against many instincts to be something they are not. A man's reaction to such an assertion is not always a pleasant one. It is difficult to want to be with someone who feels you are fundamentally flawed and if you will only do what they ask of you, then you will be acceptable. Ah, hmm . . . OK, in whose eyes?

Men hear *"you shouldn't be like you are,"* often because it's inconvenient for someone else. Men are told *"you can change,"* usually from a woman, and when a guy takes a look at himself, he really doesn't want to, nor does he see the need to change. Men are told, often with anger, *"you could if you wanted to."* I am not sure that is possible nor am I sure we want that to happen. It seems the emasculated male is no more in demand than his masculine predecessor. Perhaps it's a case of greener grass, but it would be easier if we could be ourselves. What in our shared experiences can so distort expectation from reality? Perhaps there are environmental influences which reinforce "The Promise" to make it seem more real and possible than it really is. We then ignore the real life experiences that tell our brain it's a myth and we need a better plan. Women like to think men will change. They often enter relationships believing or hoping they can. I have often discussed the concept that men are at fifty what they were at eighteen. Men change little as far as personality, responsibility, and the ability to admit failure. They change even less where initiative, trustworthiness, and honesty are concerned.

The Storybook Effect

All of us, males and females, have been influenced by the Storybook Effect. Storybook Romance novels are warm, exciting and predictable. Beautiful woman in peril meets flawed man, who, with the help of her love, sees the error of his selfish ways. He opens his heart for the first time, sees the light with the help of the woman and saves the day. They live happily ever after. We love the stories. Many believe, mostly women, some men, that these stories are what should happen. Most of us would like to believe they can really happen and that they are an actual representation of reality. But we know from experience that they are not.

What happens if a person begins to believe fairy tales are real life and believes that the Storybook model is how love is supposed to happen? If it's a man, he quickly realizes there is not a lot in real relationships that reflect that model. For women, there seems to be more difficulty breaking away from that idea and embracing a path which may lead them to happiness. Instead, the model becomes the standard from which a woman won't settle for less. OUCH . . . It's hard enough to live up to a realistic expectation let alone to a novel . . . or movie . . . or situation comedy. But that seems to be what women want. I really don't think it is, but it does get in the way of actually meeting someone who may make you happy. One annoying offshoot of believing the Storybook Model is the idea that a flawed man, with the love of a good woman, can be changed, helped to see the light and to become all that he is intended to be. That view of a man assumes there is something wrong with him to begin with. If you ask him, he will probably tell you he is fine. If you ask the woman who likes him, she will tell you if he will just (fill in the blank) he will be perfect. OMG . . . and you get married thinking that.

As humans, we seem to be divided into two camps with regard to project relationships. What is a project relationship, you ask? It is caring for someone who "needs" help, whereby the giver gains self-worth by sacrificing for another. Some have a belief that a flawed person (read "lost puppy") just needs love to be complete. The other camp tends to think of flawed individuals as potential targets to be exploited. There is a lot of pain in both camps. One is giving, over and over; the other is receiving, over and over. It also seems that women tend to view men as needing help to be what they should become. Women often seem to end up being the victims. Predators, however, are not restricted to one gender. I admire people who know going into a relationship that every day they will be working to hold together their partner. The "giver" will willingly lose his or her identity in hopes of making the other person whole. They sacrifice themselves because they love and feel they are needed. People fall into an oft repeated cycle of being with partners who they are trying to fix in the hope of finding the Storybook ending. Time after time, falling for and giving to, and being hurt . . . again and again.

While it is a part of the Storybook experience for a man to just "need the love of a good woman," it is not a part of human nature. The Storybook experience does not lend itself well to reality and the hope for a fundamental change in personality from inconsiderate jerk to a sensitive, caring, loving and unselfish partner. This is why it is called fiction. Men love science fiction in print, movies, or television. It's like a western with cool technical effects. Also, unlike romantic comedy, we don't need the hero to change for the love of a good woman. In the end, some believe Storybook novels and romantic comedies are real; however, men never believe science fiction will really happen. In science fiction (or a good western), a man can show a good side for honor, for duty, or for his friends. This represents the ideal of what men truly want to believe they can be, especially when they think of being a better man than they are afraid they truly are. Not more romantic, not more understanding but with courage, sacrifice, and with honor.

The Friend Zone

There is a place where men fear to go: it's called *The Friend Zone*. Once there, you can't get out. You can accidentally go there if you act like a friend instead of a potential boyfriend. For a woman, the Friend Zone is safe. The woman can be herself, no makeup, no dress up and no worries about sex with any male in the Friend Zone.

Women dump men by saying *"let's still be friends"* which men interpret as, *no more sex.* When a man dumps a woman using the *"let's still be friends"* phrase, it means something totally different. For a man it means *"I still want to have sex with you at my convenience,* (read Booty Call*) but want sex with other women as well."* Maybe this type of comfort level is why women often seek friendship with men and hope that love follows. For some women, a Booty Call may seem like "true love" but it's really nothing more than uncomplicated sex from a man's point of view. Booty Call, Friend with Benefits, hit and run, or ex-wife/girlfriend who allows conjugal visits, to a man it's all uncomplicated sex. These arrangements are like orgasms for free: no emotion, no time, and no financial expenditure. Men love uncomplicated sex.

The concept of not having to date, but instead, relaxing and not trying to impress one another and become friends is rampant in books, movies, and female discussions. Allowing both parties to "be themselves" is the upfront agenda but the *real* objective that many women subconsciously focus on is the Disney dream, that magic moment when eyes lock and you know, you both just know, that this is "The One." I've never seen it happen, or know anyone who has seen or had it happen, but it makes for a good chick flick. Just like playing the lottery, we are sure we won't win, but hope the planets will, somehow, align.

Men, by and large, don't become friends with women unless they have no choice. Unless a man is attracted to a women but she isn't into him, the only way to be with her is in the Friend Zone. It is that or nothing. And, once there, it's easy to believe that one day she will wake up (usually in bed with another guy) and realize it's you she really wants. Right . . . Guys, that's a clear signal to beat your head against the wall. It's not going to happen.

Why Men Date

I would like to tell you that a man dates to get to know a woman because he thinks she's interesting and that he is longing for a connected relationship and hopes that she is, too. I *would* like to tell you that, but I don't like to lie. The truth is men try to date women who they view as potential sex partners. If a man asks you out for a date, be assured that he has already decided you're a potential sex partner. Men don't really try to connect with women that they don't see as potential sexual partners unless they must for social and/or work reasons. They will try to avoid women that they don't see as bed mates. Men also realize, but usually don't admit, that they are vulnerable to women to whom they are attracted. Very vulnerable. This is more so than a man would ever admit or want to imagine. When a man views a woman as attractive, he can be influenced by the possibility of "maybe." A woman's "maybe" is the most powerful behavior influencer in the world.

The 15 Minute Rule

There is a unique inequality which exists in the world. It may be responsible for all of the differences between men and women. It has not, as far as I know, been researched but it profoundly affects male and female interactions from puberty to death. It is a very simple difference which men over the centuries have worked diligently to overcome. From patriarchal culture to behavioral psychology, untold attempts have been made to resolve it with little success. Ingrained in our genes is a significant difference which allows our species to continue, to flourish, and, at times, merely to survive. I call it "The Fifteen Minute Rule." In its simplest form, it states that every female on the planet above puberty, if she wishes, is able to have sex within fifteen minutes. Reading this, men will say, "Yes, that's right," and women will say, "No, it isn't." So let's examine The Fifteen Minute Rule in detail.

The idea of The Fifteen Minute Rule exists because men are programmed to seek sexual favor. Women have the ability to grant that favor. So, men are constantly attempting to gain favor and, therefore, sex. Most every woman I have talked with, and every woman who was honest, has confidently related three to ten men who would come have sex with her if only she would ask. They are no further than a phone call away. Now then, here's the kicker . . . it's not likely to be Brad Pitt. It's often someone with whom the woman doesn't want to have sex. The fact remains that, if a woman desires a sexual encounter with a man, she can go into a bar, the grocery store, a convenience store and hang out at the gas pump and, in fifteen minutes or less, find a man who will agree to have sex with her. That option is available to all women. To men, it is not. The role of men, as touched upon earlier, is to try to gain favor. Unlike earlier times, when women were chattel or second class citizens and passed from father to husband in an effort to maintain control, it's now against the law if a man touches a woman without her consent. We have come a long way with social order, which is good; however, the primary difference continues to exist. Men are confused by the subsequent frustrations, confusion, miscommunication, and outright indignation connected with our inability to be different than what we were genetically programmed to be. As a living species, ever with the power of intellect and reason, we are bound by those instincts which propagated the planet. We are a young species, and the drive to go forth and multiply to insure life is strong. It gets in the way of thoughtful self-control . . . a lot.

"Let's Play Dress-Up, Girls"

I remember so often being told by females, especially in gaggles (a small, bonded group of females intended for exchange of information and to form a "strength in numbers" approach to communication), that men should just be different, that we can control our urges, and that we don't have to sink lower or be gross. Females usually dress to attract attention and that isn't a bad thing. From that has evolved a very sophisticated attention management system. It is a defensive form of female behavior which is an attention seeking ploy from which reward and consequence can be delivered, depending upon who is giving the attention, i.e., if a male approaches a female who is interested in him, she smiles and eyelashes flutter. Guys with whom there is not an interest, are either patronized or for some reason receive not *"NO"* but, *"HELL NO! Go away you disgusting moron! What would ever make you think I could be interested in knowing you?"* Cool ploy, huh . . . The cards are stacked in one direction, at least from the perspective of males.

"What I wear shouldn't matter, or have an effect on men, or their behavior, or their opinion of me." That should sound familiar to most of us, either having said it (females) or heard it (males). I have often heard from women that they dress to please themselves but not men. I believe that. I

think all of us try to appear in a way that makes us feel comfortable and good about ourselves. With that in mind, let's suffice it to say that we all desire attention. We want people to like us, approve of us, and to do those things which gives us positive reinforcement. Men like color, skin, sparkle, cleavage and legs. Those things tend to draw attention, and it can be anywhere from lewd comments to glances. Along the way there are likely many undesired reactions. While bad attention is better than no attention, it is pretty safe to say there is significant difference between how responses are received, based upon the level of attraction the female has for the one reacting. The same response from one guy may be considered rude and crass while from another, funny and flirtatious. Women are very hard for men to read since men tend to be consistent in how they communicate attraction; they think women ought to be consistent as well. Silly men! This makes it really difficult to understand what a woman is really trying to say and how she wants to be treated.

So, who do people in general really dress for? People will dress in an attempt to seek the level of attention they desire. If they receive it, they are rewarded and receive positive reinforcement. If people don't get the desired reinforcement, they become more conservative or more proactive until they finally get the reaction they desire. Therefore, ladies, when you say you dress for yourselves, you're telling the truth. As long as you realize that the "you" involved is that part who seeks attention and reinforcement from others. It's not the "you" that really likes what you wear. So, ladies, for whom do you dress? You dress for yourselves . . . of course you do.

Grown Up Relationships

Most of us remember dating and pre-dating, Jr. High, PG movies, Mom and Dad, mostly Mom, talking about how it would be when we found "The One." We all had The Promise drilled into us, usually because our parents wanted us to believe in something better—something better than clumsy adolescence. Perhaps they wanted to try to manage our sexual behavior and, sometimes, because they truly believed in The Promise, even if it wasn't true for them. In looking back at those days, it seems plausible—necessary, really—that our parents actively attempted to manage our budding sexuality in a variety of ways, some good and some not so effective. For both boys and girls, one positive and not-so-intrusive way was an ongoing reference to The Promise of "The One." For girls, this was especially true due to the obvious reasons why it was deemed necessary to preserve a young girl's virginity. The Promise of "The One" gave substance to the idea of waiting for sex. Up until the sexual revolution of the 1960's and 1970's, a girl's virginity was her—and her family's—most prized asset. For boys, the continued indoctrination of The Promise of "The One" might assure that he would, eventually, choose the "right" young lady.

Historically, "The One" was a myth. Up until about the turn of the twentieth century, women were second-class citizens, even chattel, whose value to the family was minimal. In agrarian societies, once they reached child bearing age, it was time for female children to go away and reduce the drain on the family. Their value was in who they might marry. The exchange from father to husband was to be a seamless one with the woman never knowing any difference in how she was treated except for sex. It was known long ago by men, if a woman understood the power she could wield over a man who found her attractive, the balance of power would change. That is why there was an attempt to keep women chaste, virgins, unknowing. Realistically, that has never truly worked. As we have made the transition in our society from a woman being handed off from father (or other male authority figures) to husband via societal traditions such as family negotiations and agreements, matchmakers, Old World "courting," and other forms of passing females from family to family, it became necessary for males to change their techniques in obtaining a suitable mate. Hence, enter the world of modern-day dating.

Men have never really changed their dating mindset from adolescence to death. Motivation for wanting to date is pretty consistent. Techniques change with knowledge and experience but the "why" remains constant. For a woman to be successful in finding "The One," they have to understand and accept why men date. While you can yell at the wind all you want, it won't change the direction of the wind. You can want a man to be different and, for a few dates, he will be, but he will never really change. Equality of the genders socially and professionally has guided men to learn different roles to win a woman's favor. Men want a woman to like them, to bestow favor, and say "Yes." Men do what women say they should do in order to "win their hearts." Okay, after the dating and the favor and the winning of hearts and the sex, the guy goes back to being himself. All this learning the guy has picked up, and when put into action, often can be misinterpreted as lying, being a player, or participating in head games.

Take this scenario for instance: a man dates four different women in a year. Each one he goes out with he hopes will be "The One." They go out, enjoy one another, become sexual, and somewhere between the second and tenth date, it dissolves. His fault, her fault, tidal energy, who knows? It ends. If his intention is sincere and he is trying to find answers and pursue a relationship and it doesn't work, is he lying, a player, or doing head games? It would depend upon who you ask. What if it were six women in a year? What about twelve? Does that change if his intentions are sincere? We all know of circumstances when intent is not sincere and when the goal is sexual only. The lingering question remains, how to tell the difference? Now let's apply the same dating behavior to a woman. What is different? What should be? Would she deserve being considered a player, a liar, or playing head games? There seem to be different labels for women who exhibit similar behavior, but again, are they accurate? We must examine intent. Is the woman genuinely trying to find "The One" or just having fun? Is she hurting anyone, lying, or making promises she has no intention of keeping?

I think it's pretty easy for individuals of either gender to genuinely want a relationship and meander through relationship after relationship. Well, information is power so, hopefully, this discussion will provide some useful guidance. I don't think women really understand how men feel and what drives their behavior. I don't think they understand what is and what isn't important to a man when he is dating or trying to find a relationship. Some of those misconceptions cause gaps in opportunites for women. Dating truly isn't that hard unless we make it that hard.

I Don't Understand You

Friendships can develop between men and women but how they come to be is often a mystery to women. I think this is primarily because women think that men find and build friendships for the same reasons they do. And they are very, very wrong. Men have a very narrow motivation.

To understand men's primary motivations for nearly all interpersonal relationships keep in mind the old adage, *"If I don't want food or sex, I need you . . . why?"* I think it is funnier than consistently true but it makes a statement toward how men are motivated to make female connections. It also touches upon why men would be motivated to make friends of females or at least appear to become friends.

A beautiful, married woman who has many male friends often believes she is liked for her mind or her personality. That may actually be the case after a time. The question is this: would a man have talked with her enough to find out if she had a good personality if weren't for her beauty? It is possible as long as he isn't distracted by her good looks or if the situation gets uncomfortable. Generally, men can easily become friendly and, at some point, form a familiar acquaintance with a married woman. Would the man turn it into a sexual relationship if offered the choice? Let me ask the men in the crowd. Ah . . . duh!!!! While this sounds horrible and dishonorable if she is the wife of a friend, often men see sexual boundaries as primarily the work of the woman. If she wants to have a fling, and her husband won't find out . . . ok.

Women get to choose when they have sex and with whom with much greater control than men. Men's behavior is very consistent toward any woman to whom the man is attracted. Most men realize this. They know that any green light from a woman would result in a very quick *"yes."* This is regardless of the relationship between the man and that woman's boyfriend or husband. I think this is why men often seem possessive and jealous and it confuses the woman. It is because the man senses what the other men feel and how transparent the boundaries truly are. Attempts to create and maintain distance between other men to their significant other often are taken by the woman in a negative way as a matter of not trusting her. And yet, how often does a best friend end up sleeping with a wife or a husband ends up with a wife's best girlfriend? Men often don't think about it. Men just react based upon the attraction. If there is an offer for sex, *"yes"* usually comes out before the potential consequences sink in. Men, as a rule, depend upon women to set the boundaries—almost all boundaries. I know women will be upset with that, thinking that sexual boundaries shouldn't be up to them, that it isn't fair. I agree it's not fair. However, it is what it is. Again the wind analogy: you can yell at the wind, that won't change its direction or speed.

Pushing Boulders Uphill

Men and women both want the other to be different. Both men and women struggle to understand the other, and both men and women want the other to think more like each other does. Women want men to make a complex change to their genetic code through choice. That choice conflicts with not only their instinct but what they consider their best interests. Let me suggest a like trade. If a woman can do it, they have a valid and compelling argument for men to change. I would like women to not respond to situations emotionally. In a man's mind, there is no reason for not responding logically and with detachment. To borrow a female perspective: *"You could change if you really wanted to."* I think this is a good representation of the difference ingrained within us. It is difficult, if not impossible, to change just because someone else wants change to happen. It's much easier to demand a change in others when we don't really understand how deeply entrenched is the behavior. The internal drives involved in relationships push us to find safer means to our desired ends. It also drives us to erect elaborate defenses so we don't repeat mistakes, yet we often jump back in without any real difference in methods. We want to be safe, and yet we don't insure that someone likes or loves us before we give into the emotion or the instinct. Holding back isn't in the nature of men or women.

As far as change goes, no one really wants to change. Change occurs when we have to, when what we are doing is no longer working. We are forced to take a different path. If the behavior we are trying to change is genetic and not environmental, behavior modification is much more complicated if not impossible. So what do we do now?

Chapter 3

Communication
(Or lack thereof)

If you have to tell a man you are <u>not</u> High
Maintenance . . .
you are!!!

Jeremiah J. Jordan, 2011

Men are Liars

For thousands of years, women have accused men of being slightly less than completely honest. While men would deny it, is it possible that there is some truth to this belief? Do men intentionally mislead women? Do men promise one thing and deliver another? Do men present themselves in a way that is dishonest or a version of themselves which is not accurate? Well, yes . . . they do. So, the question becomes, *"Why are men less than totally honest and upfront about their intentions?"* What would motivate them to act in such a way, as to step so far out of character? What would be so significant as to take a man 180° from the direction of his socialization and upbringing? What would cause an otherwise honest man to mislead a woman in his effort to reach a desired goal and afterward not feel any level of remorse or guilt about such behavior?

It is quite confusing: a man's view of himself can be totally opposite of how he behaves where a woman is concerned. Men generally pride themselves in their unshakeable honesty in dealing with others. Men like to be thought of as being fair, direct, and most of all, honorable. Of course, there are both men and women who lie, cheat, and steal without a moment of regret; it's hard at times to tell the difference. The man a woman should want to have is willing to admit error, take consequences honorably, and continue on as best he can to improve. Men are more prone to contrition when they do wrong except when it comes to a woman. Men are consistent in behavior towards people whom they do not consider attractive or a potential intimate partner. History is littered with heroes who would gladly endure hardship, pain and suffering to help people. Yet, men will often forego their basic personality and bold face lie to a woman just because they find her attractive. The only other situation in the human condition which seems to have a similar effect would be the fight or flight reaction to fear or when the protection of a loved one is concerned. This drastic change in personal values is caused by something so very powerful because it isn't a natural condition to the person. What could possibly cause such change when a man knows it's wrong and does it repeatedly?

What motivation would apply which would alter not only socialization but basic genetic coding? Perhaps it is that genetic trump card—our instinctive drive for survival. Not personal survival as if one is in imminent danger, but that which is written into our DNA as a species. The need to procreate, at all cost. We don't feel it, don't think it, and we don't consider it. Actually, men, by and large, don't want to procreate except in certain situations. Men are, however, driven as it were, to override those thoughts, because genetics are powerful, and generally unconscious. It is what makes men and women who they are. It would be nice to think that socialization influences us more, because it fits our wants better, but all evidence seems to be to the contrary.

Women seem to want a man who is honorable, at least when they are an adult, perhaps after the age of twenty-five. A man who offers a woman the truth doesn't use her emotions to manipulate her and use her in a "hit that" and run maneuver. Thankfully, most men are honorable, generally honest, and try hard not to manipulate or use others. However, many of the attributes women are attracted to are in conflict with honor. Money, power, and possessions all erode that which is considered honorable behavior. Some professions draw men whose personalities have less than a full genetic dose of honor. I can think of several professions that, while financially rewarding, seem to be filled with the morally challenged. And yet, because of money and position, men of questionable character are able to garner affection from desirable women. So the benefit to being honest is *what* . . . exactly? Does the man get a nice person to spend time with? While it's an attractive trade off to consider, the situation is not really a "close the deal" argument. It's like, for a few dollars more I can get someone to rock my world, not just someone nice to spend time with. As men and women, our perspectives are warped by our genetics and continual reinforcement from media, friends, and our feelings.

It appears that young women are very attracted to men with type "A" personalities. Athletes, bad boys, rule breakers, and against-the-grain strong men. Oddly, those are the traits which cause these types of men to be either not reliable or unfaithful. Strong type "A" personalities tend to rationalize whatever they do as an entitlement and that's all; others are there to serve them. Consider this: if a man can lie to someone to take their money, or make a bigger profit, or slide on a contract, or advance themselves, what makes a woman think the man will tell them the truth about the significance of sex in a relationship?

People in general are pretty predictable and men in particular are very predictable. People tend to do what will help them reach their desired goal. So, if a person can't reach a goal in one way, then they will attempt to find an alternative method or route to reach the goal. If they are then successful in reaching the goal using the alternative method, they are reinforced by the success and tend to repeat the behavior. Applying that logic to the question of why do men lie may provide some insight into both men and women.

I Love You . . . Kinda

Men, by and large, like having and being in a relationship. It's more comfortable. They really do want to be with someone with whom they are attracted to and they like. They don't want to be with someone who makes them crazy. Perhaps, most of all, they want someone who is a match for their sexual desires.

Contrary to how women want the process to be, when men date, they are neither seeking a friend, nor trying to find someone to do things with or trying to find an exercise or adventure partner. Men are not seeking a soul mate, are not looking for a Storybook romance, and find no excitement in the romantic fantasy. Men do buy into the situation comedy model where a less-than-average-looking, overweight, issue-driven guy gets a very hot, smart, caring wife. It's not reality but it's a reality that men want. I have always wondered why we don't see a show depicting a frumpy, issue-driven woman with a very hot guy. We see a frumpy, issue-driven woman but her husband is often skittish or peripheral to her life. These generalizations are rarely born out in the real world, if ever. Beautiful women with an average or sub-average man brings immediate thoughts about how wealthy the guy must be or what agreement they have made. We might think that the woman must need glasses or mental health assistance. Our preferences and prejudices do come through in our observations. What we internally like and don't like come through in not only how we see other people, but how we view relationships by our judgment of those in them.

Volumes have been written about how preferences should be about the heart, what is inside, an inner beauty. It is true, to an extent, after an attraction is established. People may consider this concept to be "shallow," or perhaps shallow people think of it as "too emotional." Being truly shallow would seem to be when one seeks a partner based on how they believe others will view them instead of their own preferences. In other words, if I like red, but it benefits me in the eyes of others to like blue, I will like blue.

Men are often accused of—and guilty of—the "trophy" date/wife/girlfriend. That is, a woman who all other men desire. This is a means of trying to win or at least score points in the continuing competition amongst men. This *"see what I have and you don't"* is a continuance from the playground. Men truly never quite outgrow this competitive mindset. The woman may accept the arrangement often with some genuine feelings for the guy, at least in the short term. It must be remembered that this is a mutually beneficial relationship based totally upon want and the desire to impact persons external to the relationship. Since its foundation is externally motivated, it has no internal need or connection to keep it together past the original motivation. If he can't provide adequately, it's over; if she is no longer is an adequate trophy, she is traded in.

Men do get accused of being shallow considerably more than women, but looking at what women ask for in a dating companion gives us another perspective. A great example is a woman who desires only men eight or more inches taller. Is it a preference, a fear or security issue, or is it shallow? Women seem to get very angry when men categorize them based upon the external or physical. When men tend to view breast size or weight above being nice, the words used to describe men who do this are very non-flattering. However, when a woman has height, hair, or social-economic status as her criteria, why is it more acceptable? I know some women prefer bald men; preferences are all over the board and yes, we have to live with them. I may want a red car but if the white one has all the characteristics I want, is here now, and otherwise makes me happy, is it an "absolute" or a "nice to have?" How often does a man ask if a woman has stable employment or is financially secure?

These are walls—call them what you will—and are designed to filter out what you don't want. They are useful and designed to help you not waste your time. Preferences are part of our personality or nature. We have no influence over what we find appealing or what draws us to another. It does often make us angry what does or does not draw others to us. For instance, if a man is seeking only a slender woman, size eight or below with C cup, how would that be viewed? Many women viewing this expectation would be immediately angered by criteria so narrow and so physically weighted. I can hear it now: calling the man a pig would be the nicest thing that would be said.

What do *you* think when you see a beautiful woman with an average or less than average guy? I thought so. He must have money, right? . . . but not *he must be a wonderful person*. When we see a very handsome man with an average or less than average woman, well, that is a different thought entirely. Maybe he is helping her out, or he is a childhood friend, or perhaps he is with his cousin or sister. Let's ask this question instead: Is it possible that he could be in love with an internally beautiful person? While she may have qualities not evident to an observer, our confusion is how he could have learned about her inner beauty if his natural preference should have drawn him to a more attractive woman with similar qualities. Beauty truly being in the eye of the beholder is a good thing. It is our perception that is usually flawed. Our own perceptions reinforce that which so frustrates us with dating and relationships.

. . . and now a word from our sponsors . . .

Men and women both are affected by what they see. Often people blame advertising for leading us down a sexual path or for corrupting our moral center. Like it or not, we are influenced by what we see. Foremost, if people didn't want to see sexy things, advertisers wouldn't show them. If people weren't affected by them, they would use something else that is more effective. Sexuality is effective because it gets our attention; we can't help it. We respond. We have things which we like and don't like. And what we see is what we want to happen. Advertising or marketing taps into our wants and our fantasies. It sells books, toothpaste, and information. We are aroused by everything with the idea that "you can have this." This is a connection to our sexual person. We often want what we can't have. There are some that think that media influences thoughts and prompts less desirable behaviors. Another line of thinking is that by taking the veil away it makes things less desirable. Perhaps it works both ways depending upon the person. What should not be lost in this philosophical discussion of which came first, sexual desire or media exploitation, is that people are never convinced of a fad for long. You can promote a thing; its life expectancy is related to its ability to generate ongoing interest. Perhaps that is why sex continues to sell. If we consider why pornography, fashion, exotic dancers, prostitution, and escorts all experience great financial success even when people understand it isn't real, and that much of it is unhealthy, we perhaps can understand the impact, flirtation, and illusion of sexuality may have on men. They, by far, are the biggest contributors to the sex industry.

Men have not evolved far beyond their beginnings; it's only been 25,000 years. Men are able to discipline their behaviors in the short term if they see a reward or a consequence. Biology and genetics eventually win. As a species, we are predictably drawn to certain characteristics due to our drive for procreation. We really haven't evolved have we?

Okay, so the truth hurts but how do we deal with it?

Dating

Wasn't dating hard enough in high school and college? Nowadays it's harder. Once you reach thirty-five, if you've been married and divorced, if you have kids, or a career, and knowledge of the opposite sex, dating is harder. As grown-ups, we think we know what dating is about. We should know what is at the end of the process. We know some things about sex and communication and have done it all before. Why do we try to find a relationship and yet ignore what we have learned? Why do we try to use adolescent concepts in an adult world? Why do we think things are not what they are?

The internet age has brought about so many new ways to connect and find new and different people. The many websites devoted to finding a connection are a testament to the struggles we all have finding "The One." For both men and women, a variety of thoughts and questions might come to mind while browsing through assorted dating sites. Often, we notice key phrases that highlight profiles: "a Friend First;" "tired of games;" "looking for a Christian (male/female);" "traditional." These catch-phrases, while intended to filter potential connections, may be saying more about men, women, and dating than intended. Behind the guise of the laptop screen, it's a lot easier to "open up" about expectations and potential mates than an initial face to face encounter. That being said, why do we do such a horrible job of marketing ourselves to the available pool? Why do we believe we can have what may not exist? Why do we continue to hold out for the promise of "The One" who will make it all fall into place?

Men are different than women. No surprise there. Men are men. Toys, color, sparkle, and things that they should have long outgrown still fascinate them. The surprise comes from the idea that some people have that men can be like women and that the motives behind friendship, relationships, and dating can be the same. If you get a group of men of any age together, when they are relaxed, their behavior is not much advanced from the locker room, a parking lot, or barroom.

Women, for some reason, tend to change drastically somewhere in their mid-twenties in what they want, what they appreciate, and to whom they are attracted. That change seems to be pretty subtle but is tantamount to a woman's relationship perception. Women no longer are attracted to the adolescence in men but instead want someone thoughtful, responsible, caring, communicative, and dependable. The guys they once swooned over in high school now don't warrant the time of day from the average young woman.

A woman who is in her original marriage or relationship may not see any of this. She is living The Dream, or whatever it has turned out to be. The passage through those years has occurred and sometimes it's wonderful. Sometimes it's difficult. Sometimes she stays together for the kids or property or the hope that it will all change. If a woman isn't in a relationship, she can remember those times. Possibly she can remember or at least understand the changes that occurred in her. For that woman, the change makes for a real dilemma. She might still be longing for the bad boy but has been hurt and knows she needs the responsible guy. So, she likes to believe in the Storybook concept: a relationship with a bad boy who, with the love of a good woman (her), becomes responsible, caring, romantic, etc., etc., etc . . . ahhh. (Pounding head against wall in frustration).

Sound familiar? How does this apply to expectation verses reality? How does this affect men and women's ability to find common ground in what they want and what is real? When expectation falls short of reality, either our thinking is wrong or reality is wrong. Well, how can reality be . . . wrong? Hmmm . . . So there *is* a difference.

Is this difference real or perceptual? Do the differences between men and women mean we can't find a suitable partner? Does it mean we can't be happy? I think it really means if you are looking for a prince, he may only exist in your mind. One would think that finding a partner is a matter of setting realistic goals, moving toward them enthusiastically, and preparing and understanding what is going to happen in the process. It seems we must scout out our path to better comprehend the motivations of those we may encounter. If we can understand the motivation of an individual, we can have a good idea of not only how they will act, but how they are as a person. Remember The Promise with which we continue to struggle? The dating ideas of our adolescence we seem to drag along with us into adulthood seem to only create a mismatch between our perception of how things should be and reality. That is a really tough place to visit, let alone live. It seems many, primarily the female of the species, are putting up curtains and picking out colors.

Talk to Me!

Women are incredible communicators with one another. In a woman-to-woman conversation they tend to know exactly what each other means when they express themselves verbally. Generally, most women are able to communicate their wants, needs, and feelings and know exactly where they are in the process. Even more remarkable, women tend to know what each other means through their own, special method of communicating. Observing women communicate often makes men uncomfortable. Recall your family gatherings and what happened after the meal. Women stayed in the kitchen and men went *somewhere*—segregation. The communication patterns were on very different levels between the men and the women. For women it was very emotional, connected, familial. For men, it was often peripheral at best and more often avoidant.

Men, on the other hand, don't always read "chick speak" correctly. Okay, in truth, they *rarely* read "chick speak" correctly. Often, meaning gets lost as perception takes over. If men could only understand the romantic nature of women, of the genuine desire and whimsy in their hearts, it would be much easier to communicate, and actually be able to feel the world through that level of emotion; to understand that women truly believe in "The One," that they believe in romance, and happily-ever-after, and that women are communicating with men as *they* feel, just like they do with one another. But, men really don't appreciate a warm, loving, family-oriented woman because they don't feel it the way a woman does. They don't really enjoy long walks, or care about how close to family a woman is. They do care if a woman is friendly or smart, witty or humorous. A woman is making a marketing statement when she says "I like NASCAR," or that she enjoys dressing up and going out on occasion. You may like both, but you will generally get significantly different men to respond.

With communication we must remember that no matter how we intend another person to think or feel when they read or hear our words, they will react based upon their nature and experiences. No matter how we rant, expect, or demand, it is up to the speaker to understand how the listener perceives information. It is up to the speaker to know how to give the listener the best chance of understand what they are saying. We just can't demand that another knows. This brings me to a huge communication issue between men and women coming from that disconnect from emotions. *Men don't read minds*. Never have, never will. It is frustrating for a man to be demonized by a woman for not sensing, knowing, or feeling what it is she wants. I can recall confusion when asking that simple question, *"What do you want?"* . . . and being told, *"If I have to tell you, never mind."* If a woman wants a man to know something, she simply must tell him. If a woman expects a man to know instinctively what she thinks or wants, she is in for a lot of disappointment.

What Women Say vs. What Men Hear

The Following are quotes from dating site profiles selected because of frequency of use. If you have an online profile, you might see if any of your phrases are listed so you understand how they are perceived by men when read.

What Women Say: Part I

- I want a friend first.

- I want to find my best friend—my soul mate.

- I want to meet people—have fun.

- Nothing serious just hanging out

- Someone who shares my interests who is mentally & physically attractive

- Friend first—if it grows—awesome.

- I'm looking at just dating right now and being friends, hang out, maybe more.

- Take things slowly, become friends first.

- Someone with great personality, fun to be around, and I can talk to.

- I want someone that can sweep me off my feet

- I think you need to be friends before anything else.

- I am looking for casual dating right now.

- I want to be someone's everything.

- Someone genuine, likes to laugh, not so serious, enjoys getaways, time at lake, cares about appearance.

What Men Hear, Part I

I have been Hurt

What Women Say: Part II

- Where have the good ones gone?

- A man who isn't wrapped up in himself or work.

- A man, who is active, takes pride in appearance/work.

- I'm not looking for a relationship, friends first.

- Make a solid friend, kind, understanding and loyal.

- Have fun, not in hurry for relationship, just hang out get to know each other and enjoy life

- Looking for best friend, partner, and mate. The person I trust and that trusts me with anything.

- Honest woman seeking friend to do things with on weekends and perhaps lunch during week.

- I am looking for a companion, a friend that is honest, caring, and able to share life's adventures.

- I am looking for a man who knows how to make the women in his life feel special, treats her with respect and believes in open communication. Family values would be important to him.

What Men Hear, Part II

I have been Hurt & I don't trust men.

What Women Say: Part III

- I don't like (nor tolerate) users, abusers or cheaters in my life, so if you are one . . . Have a wonderful time with someone else, please!!!

- I don't like head games so leave me out of your life if you can't be on the up and up.

- No head games

- No players

- I'm a very simple person; no game playing

- Not looking for sexual encounters, players, or married men!

- I don't like fakes, posers or slackers

- I am looking for casual dating for now, someone to enjoy doing things together.

- I'm tired of games

What Men Hear, Part III

I have been Hurt & I don't trust men.

You will pay for what the last SOB did.

What Women Say vs. *What Men Hear:* **Part IV**

- I would also like to meet someone who knows what spontaneous is.

High Maintenance

- I want to date only Christian men who are sincere in their faith.

I have been hurt & I don't trust men.
This is my screening methodology. Oh, and no sex.

- For those of you who want a woman with a "perfect body", you might as well find someone else.

I have been hurt & I don't trust men.
I am angry that I don't look like I want to.

- All I can say is this . . . I would rather spend the rest of my life alone than settle for something less than I want, need, or deserve and you should have the same standards.

Learn to live alone and with disappointment.
Not worth investment to validate her insecurities.

- I refuse to be an option to anyone. I will be a priority to you and in your life or I will not be in your life or you in mine.

I have been hurt & I don't trust men.
Not worth investment to validate her insecurities
VERY High Maintenance

She's Got the Look . . .

There are times when a woman's appearance comes into direct conflict with the search process. Actual attractiveness, perceived attractiveness, or a complete lack of touch with reality due to attractiveness can impair the process significantly. On many dating sites the photo is as far as the man gets. Everything after is stuff. Men will read the profile "stuff" before the date if there is one. Actually, this isn't accurate; they will study it, rehearse, and find points of conversation to be able to follow the track of what the woman put in her profile. Not to mislead her—well not intentionally—just to present to her that which she will likely find favor and to better present their qualities in a light that reflects upon them positively. This happens sometimes, unfortunately, by creating positives. This gets even more distressing when we consider that depending upon the man's perception of attractiveness comes an unconscious measurement of investment in both dollars and time. This is before the date even occurs. Crudely, the woman is X cute so the man is willing to invest Y dollars and Z time until there is intimacy or he is able to determine if he wants to keep seeing her. This doesn't include issues connected with liking her or absolutes, which also become part of the mix. This process is not even conscious, but it is reinforced by male friends, as well as the marketing techniques with which we are all familiar. All of those fancy, heartfelt words from her profile are meaningless without the photo.

I think it is important to look at a few comments from women whose profile photo was exceptionally attractive to understand how a man often reacts.

- o I am looking for a friend that may grow into a romance and marriage.

This very beautiful woman will get lots of responses to her profile, but not because readers want to be friends or to know her personality or because they think she can add something to their life. This is not because she can't add to his life, but it is often a reaction driven by the attraction, and a rush to connect, with a willingness to find out about the woman, as long as sex is involved.

- o I think a good relationship starts with a good friendship, with no drama . . . I think family is very important.

This is from a beautiful woman who will receive a great many responses. Each response will try to reflect as closely as possible to exactly what she said she wanted. Most of the men responding having little to no concern for her as a person. The concept of family for a man is quite different than a woman's. Hanging out with family is either a big *yes* or a big *no* . . . depending upon the family.

- o I am smart, attractive and self-sufficient. I work full time and support myself quite comfortably. I want a man that can tame this independence.

This was written by a very attractive woman almost to the point of being intimidating. Further emasculation is proclaimed by boasting self-sufficiency. It's nearly a challenge. An "A" type personality would take that challenge, play for a while and after they felt they had won, would move on. The mixed message nearly assures that no matter which angle the man takes, it's wrong. Any man who has a chance to make her happy would not meet her physical requirements or get past her defense mechanisms. Most any man that did measure up would be there for their pleasure or ego not a relationship and will leave at the first sign of emotional cost.

The following is paraphrased from a profile and comments come from male reactions to it. Consider these things to avoid during the marketing process for a relationship.

- I have spent the biggest part of my adult life alone. I am ready to find the one to spend the rest of my life with.

    Don't say you have spent a lot of time alone. Men realize there is a reason.

- I like the same things everyone else does . . . sunsets, the beach, holding hands, snuggling on the couch, long walks, etc.

    Men don't like these things unless it leads to sex

- I am looking for that person that makes me want to get up in the morning, can't wait to get home and see him and feel myself wrapped in his arms, to know that no matter what happens he will be there to protect me from the cruel world.

    zzzzzzzzzzzzzz sorry what?

- I want to find my best friend, that person that I feel so comfortable I can sing, dance, and be silly. I want to feel like a school girl, I want to shout from the rooftops.

    Sing dance, right zzzzzz

- Not interested in older men, (men older than her age minus 10 years)

Relook at pic . . . hmmmmm, Likes playthings, not relationships, or being a short term plaything for a young man wanting an older women experience. Cougar.

o   Man may be financially stable or rich for that matter.

Telling me money and status are important.

o   I am attracted to tall (5'10" or taller) men,

She is 5'2" she wants 8" difference? What issues does she have, daddy, protection?

o   Men that are not over 52-53 years old

Review her photo again. A very narrow group for 50-ish women who is not really "all that" let alone with no bag of chips.

o   No alcoholics or taking any kind of mind altering anti-depressant drugs.

Recovering or active? Wonder if she has bias against diabetes or other medical conditions. What else is on her list of unacceptable that she isn't talking about?

o   I am a very strong woman and am quite capable of taking care of myself

Ok, there's the threat.

o   I may "look" high maintenance; I feel that it is the little things that you do that endear you in my heart.

You don't look high maintenance, you sound extremely high maintenance. Many, many little things over and over. A simple rule for men: if a woman has to say she isn't high maintenance, she most definitely is.

- I have a picture up and ask that you please do the same . . . No picture . . . No response from me. Look at my picture and then go look in the mirror, I do not want to date someone that looks 20 yrs. older (grandpa) than me.

  Somewhat attractive woman—a 5 or 6 now. Once was very attractive I am sure . . . now lined, average figure no quality options visible, can see a lot of mileage . . . looks older than her age, inability to self-evaluate and expectations much higher than market value would indicate possible.

- I have been doing this dating thing for 10 years.

  No kidding, have you ever wondered why?

- I have just about had my fill of it, so please, someone, show me that there actually are some real men out there.

  With all the issues presented, men likely will drift in, enjoy, and drift out, if they drift in at all. One can hear the nagging tone in the profile. For her, real men must be men who actually don't behave like men because the men she is wanting don't exist in reality.

- Men that want their best friend . . .

  See why men date: Chapter 2

- . . . as well, and can "hang" with someone and be friends first . . .

  Repeat: See why men date: Chapter 2

- . . . and watch love bloom . . .

  gagging . . .

It is no wonder this woman has been alone for years. She doesn't understand the men to whom she is trying to appeal. She isn't really attractive enough to get the selection of men she is marketing toward since that man wants to spend his time with someone more attractive and less caustic than she. She also opens herself up to men who are serial monogamists. Comes, dates, enjoys, and leaves when the woman becomes annoying, he is bored, or something else catches his fancy. If you create such an unfriendly image of yourself, it's difficult for anyone—shallow or not—to see you as worth the effort. Once a woman is seen in a way where her sexuality isn't worth the energy it would take to enjoy it, the woman might as well enjoy being alone. That situation doesn't provide any motivation for the man to take her out or see what might happen. This is neither overt cruelty in the man nor is it really that unusual a marketing concept for the women. We all are driven by attraction, no matter what we tell others when we want them to see us less selfish than we truly are. It is also a characteristic in us to which we may not want to admit.

Take careful aim at your foot and fire . . .

These comments, expectations, and wish lists were all written with the best of intentions and with hope. When taken as a whole it's rather overwhelming. What do these many sentiments have in common? They were all in women's profiles, written by thousands trying to find a relationship. I didn't select a sentiment unless I found it over twenty times. That usually meant looking at twenty-two profiles. The request to be "Friends First," so as to protect oneself, is a simple enough and reasonable request, yet the basic problems men and women have with one another still exist. Men similarly shoot themselves in the foot profile wise, but since men date with different intentions, their standards aren't as high. Men can afford to be shoddy. The internet brings to us sheer numbers that are thrown into the pool, so there will be even more people with whom you don't understand nor do they understand what you mean.

Yes, these examples were written by women, obviously nice women, wanting to find a nice man for a relationship. Let's chat, meet, become friends and see what happens. Other than my telling you, how would you know it was a woman who wrote these descriptors? A man would never say these things unless he was trying to impress a woman with how in tune he was to her. Internet dating has become the new acceptable way to find a relationship—which is great. Female profiles are full of phrases like these that state over and over how little women understand men, which is not great. Those phrases also make a statement about how little a woman knows about what powers the relationship engine. To that end, I know women want a certain "thing" in a relationship and in a man. It would be even better for women if the "thing" they want men to be actually existed in real life. If it did, why didn't they find it the first time? I guess it makes more sense to hold on to that sliver of hope that a man like she wants actually exists and that she can continue to cling to "The Promise."

Sadly, many men work hard to play along with this type of female whimsy if the candidate's photo depicts her as being attractive, at least in the eye of the beholder. Men are well trained. Men are conditioned at an early age how to respond to a female. Tell her what she wants to hear. Men do what they think they have to do to make a woman like them. *"Sure, I want to be a friend first."* he says sincerely, but follows up with what he thinks she wants to hear: *"I really want to go slowly and get to know one another."* If you hear these words coming from a man's mouth, you can be pretty sure he is either not interested in a relationship with you or he is lying. Not a BIG lie, just a little white lie. He's not trying to take advantage of you; he's just trying to make you like him. So he tells you what you want to hear. That little white lie is his first technique to achieve his initial goal of gaining your confidence in him.

Of course, sex is the ultimate goal. Again, the little lie is not evil, just a ploy to achieve his aim—to have sex with this attractive object of his desire. There are some things that must be accepted about men. They are shallow and their first reaction stems from a visual cue. If it looks good, give it a shot. When a man asks a woman out on a date, he is attracted to her and has deemed her a potential sexual partner because he saw, literally, something about her that attracted him.

Jeremiah J. Jordan

The Power of Maybe

How do I know women don't really understand men? Women believe in "The Promise." They feel men should have evolved to want them as a result of something other than physical. I know this because a woman has the greatest human power on earth and doesn't appreciate it nor use it to her advantage. The power comes from the simplest of places. Not a deed or action but a mere hint of a suggestion. The simple word . . . *maybe* is the source of nearly unlimited power. *Maybe* . . . the thought that *maybe* she likes me, or *maybe* she will. That *maybe* is what drives men to launch a thousand ships, to write poems, to sing songs, and be stupid. Unfortunately for women, *maybe* is temporary, it goes away with time and the influence wanes because of familiarity and achievement of the goal (*read* sex). But a woman's *maybe* will always drive men. *Maybe she will?* Men don't even have to know what "she will" means. Generally it's just maybe she will like me. Color, sparkle, skin, smiles, a touch on the arm, all make men really stupid. Ladies, you don't have to act on the *maybe*, but it is what gets you in the game and can keep you there—at least long enough to decide if you want to keep him. You should have learned how to use all of your skills to achieve a task. *Maybe* is one of them; a harmless skill unless evil intent is attached. Malevolent forces are out there, as well. As eloquently said years ago, "*you can attract more flies with honey than with vinegar.*" A smile and the possibility of something pleasing will always trump having a rock thrown at you.

How Did We Get Here?

As an adult, I miss the hope that was present when I was a teenager and dating. There was always excitement and anticipation of what might take place. Adults back in the dating scene seem to be missing that hope, that anticipation of things to come, the excitement of getting to know a new person. In younger days, we often already knew the person involved and may have been acquainted for many years. Sometimes, a date—the proverbial "blind date"—had been set up for you by well-meaning friends. Or maybe you experienced that intense draw to someone you thought was cute. Perhaps there was that aching fear and terrible beauty of the possibility of a first date and the mixed feelings of joy and despair that came with either a *yes* or a *no*. The long walk across the gym floor at the high school dance and the anticipation between boy and girl and the awkward smiles that came with thinking about the first kiss and the newness of it all were overwhelming. *You dreamed about the excitement and wonder of this first intimacy and the hope of falling in love and of being loved. You hoped that this special person was "The One."* Later, after graduation, after college, after starting that first job, we went into that first marriage with those hopes and dreams of adolescence. Later, we grew up. Things changed. We learned.

Maybe we learned too much

If we are alone and still dating after, say age thirty-five, if we have been in a marriage, or a relationship, for longer than a year before it dissolved, there are some things we must accept as we try to move forward. We know something happened. We have opinions about what happened. We were affected by what happened. We just aren't sure how we were affected and how it will influence our moving forward. That will depend upon what actually went wrong. Rarely do people enter into a relationship, especially a marriage, knowing it is temporary. We all have had a dream. We all wanted to live it. Something was wrong or we still would be living that dream.

We made the wrong choice in partners

We were too young, they changed, or they didn't change. They got strange, quit listening, weren't the person we thought they were, and lied to us. They didn't grow up, were no longer fun, didn't enjoy the same things, were irresponsible and couldn't communicate. Whatever the reason, we chose poorly. Along with that came several deeply entrenched feelings which pop up from time to time when we date. People do or say things that remind us of our previous poor choices. We run away, block off our emotions, and stop what we are feeling as best we can. While we call them *"Red Flags,"* they are the scars left to us by our trust being violated. The person may not have those traits, but that awareness makes us discard them and the person they are. We will paint the person with the broad brush of our former relationship making it difficult to really see who we are with. We sometimes are accused of choosing our parents: sons pick their mothers, and daughters pick their fathers. This is an understandable connection to accept, unless there is an unpleasant relationship existing in the parent-child dynamic. There is the idea that we would prefer the hell we know to the heaven we don't know. We're often too afraid to address unpleasant issues, fearful of the pain it would cause, thereby continuing to live miserably rather than taking the chance to embrace a happier life. For whatever reason, the most common answer given by women as to why their marriage or long term relationship fails is they chose badly. Carrying this idea that we chose badly affects future decisions significantly, especially if a person keeps making errors in selection. We may have to date a lot. Often we get our feelings hurt. Often the person we like turns out to be different than the one we believed they were. Should this be a criticism of them not being honest or of our not paying attention?

You Have Three Options

In committed or connected relationships (not necessarily marriage but relationships where the parties feel they are in love—however it's defined), it is often suggested that communication, or the lack of it, is the reason for failure. Oddly, people are very good at telling others how they feel and what they want. People communicate pretty well. People who are together usually have many ways of expressing themselves. Many times it's clumsy, erratic and inconsistent, but we express ourselves. The problem with communication is when one person states his or her needs and the other either doesn't care, doesn't listen, or ignores it. Once that has occurred, the erosion of the relationship begins. Once one member of the relationship feels their needs are not being met, once they have expressed themselves clearly and nothing has changed, once they have passed the point of reasonably believing the other will change, they have three options. Only three. No more.

The **First** option is that they can leave. Understand that this is a considered option, but not a desired one and it rarely occurs, even when the person knows things won't get better. Fear of failure, family, faith, (*"you made your bed now sleep in it"*) and other kinds of excuses people use to stay in hopeless situations. Why is it hopeless? It is hopeless because the relationship we had hoped for is not to be. It is hopeless because the relationship we believed we were getting and what we actually have are so different. It will not recover, trust is broken, and contempt, anger, and frustration are reinforced daily. Kids, debt, and fear of failure cause people to stay, among other things. Even sadder is that this situation will fall inordinately upon females. They seem to find themselves in a "no hope" situation more often than men. There is no surprise that there is an ongoing impact upon women in their post-breakup relationship efforts. Communication wasn't the original problem; it was with whom they chose to put their faith. Communication is ultimately blamed and it becomes a big issue in ongoing dating and relationships. It is what causes the perceived need for the "Friends First" strategy to be such an ongoing and self-defeating mindset. It is much more comforting to think poor communication by the man was the problem instead of accepting the possibility of one's own poor decision making. You can't blame *yourself*, now, can you?

The **Second** option is to accept with joy in your heart the situation and be thankful. I have heard many people, mostly women with children, say they will do this. Often it is labeled as a faith builder, to pray for change, which, oddly, doesn't ever come. They have kids, they have family, will suck it up, expect less, and go on. Remember all the times we hear someone say they won't settle again? This is engrained into us by our succumbing to this mindset. I will accept my burden, my choices, and put a bright face on it. While people believe they make this choice and actually do it, the second option is impossible. It's impossible primarily because every day they are reminded of the problem, of how their feelings and needs are not only not being addressed but how unimportant their feelings and needs truly are and how unimportant they are to someone to whom they gave their youth, their hope, and most of all, their dream. It is brutal and continuous and wearing. It is no wonder why dating is so hard later on.

The **Third** and most selected option is to find an alternative means, generally external, to get one's needs met. Intentionally or unintentionally, people will find ways to make themselves feel good about them and to find a way bolster their self-esteem, to feel loved or needed or wanted. These ways can include focus on children, work, and volunteering. These are the more positive ones but all are temporary and time diminishes the amount of reinforcement received. We often see when the kids leave, a job changes, or anything leaves the couple together alone (or maybe "together" but altogether *alone*), the relationship quickly dissolves. In this scenario it ends because of years of exhaustion and indifference, and most often in a whimper. However, alternative means of reinforcement can also lead to alcohol, drugs, flirtation, sexual affairs, and a complete deviation from one's personality. This leads to not only relationship distance and ultimately breakdown, but also guilt, frustration, or depression. A relationships ending as a result of one of these is usually more abrupt and occurs in a very ugly way. This also carries very deep impressions upon potential future relationships. Understand that in both instances the relationship was already gone, just the players remained in place.

Eventually, people get back to the first option. It probably would be better if they would have done that initially, but we don't or can't or won't. It is devastating to us and nearly debilitating to our future. We made a bad choice; we live with it instead of cutting our losses and moving on. It makes finding happiness harder. And, by the way, say "thank you" to all those external voices which goaded, proselytized, and shamed you into the ongoing pain. Aren't these the ones you still listen to and seek their approval. And how is that working for you now?

We were the wrong choice

It is difficult for our egos to come to accept that *we* were the wrong choice for someone else. We don't want to think that could happen. We almost never can believe we could be the wrong choice. Partners find others, leave for other reasons. It's always *their* fault, *their* shortcomings, *their* weakness. We made the wrong choice, not them. Often, men leave first wives for a younger model. Women leave their husbands for a more successful model. These are generalizations and stereotypes which are not always true and, in reality, are often only in our minds, yet we openly express them and believe them to be true. We have trouble accepting that the wrong choice was us and that we weren't or aren't enough. In can be the result that, while we were not flawed, the other person just wanted something else. They made the wrong choice. We are much more comfortable beating ourselves up about it rather than seeing we never could be happy with someone who wanted something different. As a result, it keeps us from being able to give ourselves totally to almost anything. The weight of the fear in wondering *"what if we commit 100%, give all, and it isn't enough?"* What does that say about us? It says many good things but all we understand is *we aren't enough.*

The old saying *"you have been weighed, you have been measured, you have been found wanting"* is an expression of failure. I have heard many people use this saying incorrectly, interpreting that if you are found wanting, you have failed completely. This also makes an assumption that the person doing the measuring was measuring the right thing, using the correct ruler or knew what significance the standard held. They are not only mistaken in interpretation but harmful to those they convince to believe them. Yet, it doesn't tell us about effort or about how close we came. It doesn't remind us that while we weren't a right fit for one thing we are a right fit for so many others. This is one of many well, or not so well, intentioned and severely misguided attempts to use a very complex concept to make a simple point in an effort to manage another's behavior. It often means instead of weighing 26 pounds it weighs 25 pounds and 15 ½ ounces. This thinking assumes we are on a Pass/Fail System as opposed to being graded. If the expression stated that we had been found wanting with regard to the minimum acceptable standard we would have more clarification. What if we got a 99 instead of a 100? The saying is applicable to either since there is no clarification. In human terms, we hate to be found wanting at anything, but we often are. Sometimes it's us, sometimes it's the other, and sometimes we will never know. Also, when it comes to being found wanting by another, it is usually an arbitrary decision. It is one person's opinion. You may think you love that person, but it is a self-serving and biased observation. We are as quick to view a glimpse of failure as total failure, so we don't try, we don't accept, we don't realize it's alright if someone else chose wrong. We could never be really happy in a relationship in which our partner wanted something else. Not better, just something else.

You had a loss

A significant loss, such as losing a partner through death or divorce, the loss of a child, losing a job or failing in a business endeavor—any loss and the grief and trauma associated with it—can affect our ability to see people clearly and to make smart choices. Losing a partner, in any manner, can significantly affect dating and relationships in general. It is difficult, if not impossible, to replace a partner from a long term relationship. The memory of "The Other" is enhanced by the loss of that person and the apparent differences between the former beloved and a new beloved would be apparent. It is hard to erase the memory of a loving relationship, even if it was flawed. When a former relationship scars a person, issues of insecurity can surface and cause damage in the new relationship. When we have been hurt by another, we blame them and are simultaneously filled with shame that we may have caused the difficulties. Until we can move past the blame/shame cycle, we cannot get beyond the person we lost to allow for healthy emotions to develop. We will "carry the torch" of the pain from the past into any new relationship until we can let go of the past and accept we were not for them.

Since grief is cumulative and pervasive, each loss building upon the last, we carry around all losses with each new one. It takes a lot of time and thought to overcome anything which prompts that level of sadness. In trying times, where there is uncertainty in our work, health, or life situation, it makes opening ourselves emotionally difficult if not impossible. The grief from a loss combined with fear and insecurity makes for a disturbing combination. Sadly, people often find themselves in this situation just when they are also trying to find an enduring relationship. No wonder it's easy to make poor choices. It's is hard enough to make the right choice when we are emotionally healthy and secure. For men, losing a job can be tantamount to losing the sense of self. All the things they have been taught to be, and how to measure themselves, are suddenly gone. At times when men most need a partner they are the least equipped to find the right one and most likely to make a poor choice.

Losing family or anyone close for any reason is always difficult for people. We lean upon our partner during those times. If the relationship is already in distress or dissolving, the impact of a loss is much greater on the relationship and contributes to resentfulness. It is so very easy to shift the grief from our loss to underserved blame toward our partner. Not necessarily for what they did but for what they couldn't do to make us feel better. For any loss, families and friends seem to have a 50/50 impact upon a loss or grief experience. Half of them do try to be helpful and supportive to the individual immediately following the loss. This has to be in the manner most comfortable to the giver of support than to the grieving. People always want to give support as long as they can limit the amount and kind of support. This is still a huge amount in proportion to the other half who doesn't extend support at all.

The Death of the Dream

Those of us growing up with The Promise are doomed to always have a trace of it in our psyche. Success, joy, happiness, and "The One" constantly touch our minds and hearts. That is why we enjoy books and movies about romance and "happily ever after." They bring to us some contact with that for which we yearn. There is a part of us that so wants it to be true. There are very few times in our lives when we feel both in love and loved and where there is complete security in our relationship as well as an overwhelming need to be connected to another. As teenagers we often feel that intensity, but the object of that intensity is often fluid. Puberty isn't very kind to our emotions. As adults, we recreate that state of euphoria and we hope that "The One" actually exists that creates that dream in us. Happily. Ever. After.

As a grown-up, if we have had that first marriage fail, no matter under what circumstances, we must deal with the grief which comes from the death of our childhood dream. We will always feel a little tarnished and somewhat lessened by the failure. While it never was real, The Dream was motivating to us during our most developmental years. It created a mindset in us that determined if we were successful in a relationship or not. It created a measurement for us to judge ourselves, no matter what the problems were in the relationship. You either succeeded or you didn't. No matter how badly the first one ended, it didn't matter if you went from a bad relationship immediately into a great one. The Dream—which came from The Promise—died and our grief over the loss of it influenced how we proceeded into the rest of our lives.

Jeremiah J. Jordan

Perspective from Pain

An old friend of mine, Robert Dolezilek, once said, *"This is a world of diminishing firsts."* It takes a while to understand how that can influence our decisions but once we have experienced something, we can't help but approach it differently the next time. In our society, and perhaps our species, we revere experience for all but relationships. We don't think highly of anyone who has multiple relationships, or at least not openly. Men are envious of other men with multiple sexual relationships but women find this to be abhorrent. We celebrate longevity but not experience. We give an award for tolerance but not exceptionalism. A couple who hates one another but stays together for fifty years gets a big party but a couple that has an incredible five years together where they were both happy and grew but it changed, and they parted as friends, are chastised for giving up. This logic again goes back to The Dream, finding "The One." Additionally, it upsets the control of the social order if people are relationship fluid. The patriarch will always fear it will be his possession—I mean wife—that finds a better deal and subsequently leaves.

The death of The Dream may affect our choices for the next relationship because we may never feel worthy again. Or we may believe we need to be punished. We don't deserve happiness. That would explain a lot of the poor choices people make with regard to whom they choose to be connected. There is also the hostility, often covered over, toward that which hurt us. The easiest way to feel better about one's self is to make another feel bad. Sometimes, after being emotionally damaged, we can feel it necessary to hurt others to regain our power or inner balance. Revenge is a huge motivator, even if it is directed toward a gender instead of the person who did the hurting. Generalized anger is common when emotion is connected. We like to own the feeling of entitlement that it's acceptable to hurt or use another because of one's own pain. We get very selfish when we have been emotionally injured. We lash out, we do damage, and we feel guilt which leads to more poor choices in order to make amends. We struggle onward to find "The One" never considering they exist only in our dreams.

Chapter 4

Grown Up Relationships

Elevate yourself to something better than you are. Coupling is comfortable—sometimes for fifty years, sometimes for fifty days. Both are a blessing to us. It means that someone cared for us and we cared for that someone, if only for a short time. We cannot predict how long any relationship will last, we can't control everything. We have a divine chalice we bring to a relationship. We do influence others as to what they take away from their time with us. We get so few chances that it is sad people squander them instead of embracing those opportunities. We are better served when we make the best of them.

Jeremiah J. Jordan, 2011

Isn't that Special?

All of us want to be special. One enduring aspect of human interaction is the idea of uniqueness. People express how their particular circumstance is unique or how it is much more significant than that of the rest of the world. We protect the idea of our own uniqueness by resisting being grouped with others and yet we compartmentalize others as much as possible for our own benefit. An aspect of our diverse and complex social structure is the desire to identify a small fragment of a concept instead of the larger generalization. In other words, we generalize others while at the same time we are overly compartmentalized with ourselves. This allows us to think of ourselves outside of any group we have identified. We remain unique. When examining the components of successful adult relationships, many who write or speak on the subject seem to break them down into many tiny, separate parts. While these overly specific slivers of significance provide for a great deal of food for thought, they generally make understanding more confusing. Identifying the many small things which determine a relationship's success can make us all feel more important since we happen to struggle with a specific one. People often can use a very narrow hypothesis to make sense of their particular circumstance but when it's generalized with others it often doesn't quite fit.

KISS

Using the KISS principal as a guide, (Keep It Simple Stupid), it seems appropriate to review the thousands of ideas about the parts of relationships which people have identified. A look at the many components of what makes relationships work or not work yielded what seems to be a very simple approach to adult relationship success. After all that filtering, we can come up with four aspects of a grown-up relationship which seems to be constant and from which all the pieces can be grouped. There are four things which must be present for a relationship to begin and to continue. These four things—*which must exist*—might be considered prerequisites because if any one of them is missing, the relationship fails. Always fails, no exceptions. If we view our past relationships and are honest with ourselves, we can find at least one which ceased to be and how things fell apart. Let's examine the four basic, but essential, components to a relationship.

Jeremiah J. Jordan

Attraction—Connection—Absolutes—Sex

These four elements are not much of a surprise when we look at them. We can easily apply them to our relationships or to those we know. If these four components are all in place, a relationship survives and, perhaps, flourishes. If they are present, no one wants to leave. If any are missing, it dissolves . . . always.

Attraction

It is no mistake that attraction is first on the list. When we consider what attraction is to our species, we ultimately have to admit it's about with whom we want to have sex. We would probably prefer to think we are past all that and there are other attributes which apply. We can point to relationships which have nothing to do with sex that seem to do fine, at least we think so. There are always unique circumstances which don't follow the rule but, by and large, we are driven by our basic instinct more than our disciplined thinking. It's an involuntary reaction which has to do with our biology. It is driven by our will to survive and procreate. And, even after we are no longer able to reproduce ourselves, attraction to the opposite sex continues to influence us.

Attraction continues to influence men long after their desire to procreate or their ability has diminished. Attraction has nothing to do with good sense or good choices. If it did, we would only be attracted to people with good character. What we have to look for in a partner—what is inside—runs quite contrary to how we are wired. This is especially true for men, but both men and women find attraction as the driving force in relationship decision making. The physical aspects of attraction are evident in all humans. Pupils dilate, our posture changes, we get more animated. I guess it's the process of wanting to be noticed or that extra dump of adrenaline into our system that does the trick. If we look at animals in the wild, males trying to attract females have their own types of body language and posturing to attract a potential mate. Men affected by attraction are pretty silly to observe. It is embarrassing to be one of the several males caught staring like junior high boys at a pretty woman.

The same goofy looks are there, and if she spoke to any of them, the same tongue tied responses can be heard. There is nothing like forty-plus men doing backflips to entertain or interest a potential mate as she smiles, feels assured, then wanders off with a knowing smirk on her face. It is apparent that our genetics have caught up with us.

We know that attraction has nothing to do with what's inside someone. It does, however, have a lot to do with how we respond to people and how we are affected by those to whom we are attracted. Men don't have to like a woman to be attracted to her. Men actually can despise a woman and still be extremely attracted to her. If we reflect upon the choices we have made relationship-wise, we might be able to assess how attraction has played into those choices. Women do have it right—it is about what is inside a person that makes a relationship work. There are very few of us that make the connection when we are young of how important the substance of a person is to the success of a relationship. Our youth and lack of awareness allows for a relationship to take on a "Oneness" quality that seems to be a romantic journey to an observer. That connection with the inner part of another in our youth is often an illusion perpetuated by the couple. It's a little like a fairytale that gives us hope for ourselves and our chance for happiness.

What appears to be the biggest difference between men and women are our views toward sexuality and how they affect relationships. It is generally accepted that if a man finds a women attractive he will willingly engage in sexual behavior with her. For a woman, that connection to attraction isn't as clear. For a relationship to exist, especially an adult relationship, attraction must exist. That is, one can see themselves being sexual with the other person. If that doesn't exist, then the relationship is a different one than traditionally thought of as romantic. For men in particular, this is generally an undesirable situation as long as the potential for sexual behavior exists.

Perhaps that is why men don't see themselves clearly as far as how they are perceived by women. Men tend to think they look great no matter what and that a woman should want to be with them. Women, on the other hand, tend to be overly critical, often not seeing themselves as attractive.

Men don't understand that or any excuse that interferes with the moment. If a man is attracted to a woman, location, dress, level of personal hygiene, current reproductive situation, or verbal rejection will not deter his desire. Recently, during a discussion group, a woman was confused that men would find her attractive after they learned she was married. She believed that being married should eliminate other men's attraction or sexual desire for her. As many can attest to, that isn't the case. Marriage does bring with it some advantages for a woman with the attraction or unwanted attention issue. This is a ready-made reason to send an unattractive man and his attention down the road: him knowing that she is "taken" and her using her relationship status as a weapon to deflect the unwanted and undesirable male. However, this in no way deters men from pondering "what if" and in some instances enhances the thought. We are often desperate to want what we shouldn't have, especially if it belongs to someone else.

We must always remember that we cannot control or even significantly affect another person's thoughts or feelings and, only in some cases, their behavior. We must understand that a person's instincts weigh far heavier on their decision making process than their thinking process. To some, just because we shouldn't do a thing means we shouldn't think of that thing. As most of us know, it takes incredible discipline to overcome our basic instincts. Air, food, water, shelter, and sex are well identified as basic needs of our species. When any of them are denied, it can create anxiety and often desperation in the individual. This self-denial can influence one's ability to interact in a meaningful way with another person and to be able to function successfully in a relationship. We must accept our feelings as they are since they can't be controlled by intellect or will. We can have limited influence on our thoughts. While we may have some luck managing our thinking through forced denial, guilt and recrimination, often that makes us more vulnerable to the original thought. The only things we can control are our choices and subsequent actions.

We can't help who we are attracted to and usually have trouble explaining to others why we are enamored with the object of our desire. If others can't see it, then our explanation does little to help. Attraction isn't always easy to understand, and it can appear to be in a constant state of flux. We are often affected by mood, or whim, or just because our preferences often vary. If one looks carefully at anyone with whom they are attracted, they can find flaws or reasons not to be attracted. Generally speaking, this is very effective in reducing the impact of the attraction. It does take effort to look for the flaws; it is much more desirable to go with the fantasy.

While we cannot control to whom we are attracted, there are situations where that attraction can brings feelings of disloyalty or are a little too unsettling. Many of us put into place ways to fool ourselves. This is a method used by both men and women and, while contrary to our basic programming, it can be learned. A habit can be developed through repetition for finding fault to diminish our attraction for others. Once established, because of commitments, fear, or compliance, it is very hard to flip the switch back. It becomes a part of the senses to be so critical as to eliminate all comers because of flaws. I believe this happens often with people who spent a long time fighting natural attraction toward others. This is good behavior if you are in a committed relationship; however, once this becomes habit, if or when the relationship falls apart, it continues to cast negatives upon anyone who comes along with whom there is an attraction. In other words, whenever we feel an attraction that we don't want, we automatically look for that which will diminish it. Additionally, we have to consider that if our relationship was what it was supposed to be, we easily could have appreciated the attractiveness of others while still maintaining desire and connectedness to our partner. It is only when we struggle within a relationship or have feelings that are less than what we want or need them to be that we have to force ourselves to "not look." Perhaps if we would have addressed the original problem, looking wouldn't be a problem at all.

For men, attraction can be forced upon them to some extent. A woman's voice, smell, and often color, shine, or sparkle can get a man to notice. Dress, posture, and the little bit of cleavage a woman presents can carry a lot of weight as far as attraction. While these are temporary and fleeting, they do create an opportunity. A man can focus upon a single attribute in a woman which makes her desirable and this can make him virtually unable to resist her. Again, this is temporary; however, women have successfully used any number of "attractive devices" for years as a means of getting attention. This behavior can garner attention anywhere from flirtation for flirtation's sake to deriving a sizeable income. The only salvation a man has and possibly the only way he can cope is that he becomes quickly and easily bored with this type of behavior.

There is a situation which I think is more often associated with men than with women. Men are often attracted enough to play but not to stay. This is one aspect of male attraction and behavior and it is one that women would like to eliminate. This viewpoint may not be possible because of how men view women as potential sexual partners versus how they view potential relationship partners. I do believe it is within a woman's power to understand her power of attraction and utilize that skill for her benefit. Women have been doing that since we lived in caves—attracting men. Accepting the reality of male behavior and utilizing knowledge will allow the women to better navigate through dating to relationship waters. Subsequently, if a man is attracted enough to *play* but not attracted enough to stick around, perhaps something else is missing. There must be a connection between him and her.

Connection

If it is the attraction that brings us to one another it is the connection that keeps us there. Connection is about liking a person. It is about enjoying someone's company. It is the "click" between two people. Admiration can also be a part of the mix in a relationship, although it may not always be so, both individually as well as mutually, but it is a huge connecting mechanism. Some thinking on relationships presumes a simple idea: if mutual admiration doesn't exist then how can a couple connect in a meaningful way? What if one doesn't admire the other but they have sex anyway? Does this mean that "you won't respect me in the morning?" Maybe there really isn't a connection without true admiration. This implies a perceptual equality between the partners in the couple. There is some conceptual truth in this but not as clearly as it first appears. While there is a degree of commonality in the qualities that the sexes admire in one another, there are often quite different attributes that each admire in the other. A man wants a woman to admire him for his prowess, work, skills, and ability to succeed. He may very well admire a woman for her physical attributes, social skills, organizational ability, home management and emotional connections—the things he wishes not to deal with. Men admire qualities in a woman they don't see in themselves, and it is likely similar with women. We often admire in others what we see lacking in ourselves. We must also remember that admiration is just a short emotional drive to envy—an emotion that sits on the outskirts of jealousy. A man and woman may enjoy and respect each other's values, belief system, social skills, work ethic, etc. Couples may have mutual admiration for similar things about one another and, while this may not always be true, differences can still be workable and useful toward liking and wanting to be with someone. As long as we believe we are admired for what we think we are admired for, maybe it doesn't matter what is truly being admired.

That you like to be with someone and that they make you feel good about being with them is very important to our self-esteem. Often, when couples no longer enjoy being with one another for any reason, the relationship becomes difficult if not impossible to continue. Since connection is what helps a couple through difficult times, and is the glue when other aspects of the relationship may diminish, it can't be minimized. Connection determines how stable, secure and enduring a relationship will be. People, especially women, want this to develop first. Men want this to develop last, after considerable time, interaction, and testing. Whether because of early dating or genetic composition, men are very unwilling to open themselves to the deep non-physical intimacy of a true friendship with a woman. Perhaps because of the inherent weakness men have for women with whom they are attracted, they are hesitant to be emotionally open. For a man, that is what a friendship with a female is: emotional dependency upon his partner for support, for assurance, for clarity, for ego bolstering, for staying the course. A man can do those things but it takes a lot of energy and men thrive on exterior means of reinforcement. Men truly want to be loved; however; it's a slow process to get them there. Men want the same end that women desire. It's a leftover from "The Promise" still running through their heads. The journey and things which affect men and women along the way are not the same, but the goal is the same. In general, we think of men as more risk taking and women as the sensible ones. Men often depend upon their female partner for being sensible. It follows then that women want a reasonable assurance of a safe landing before they jump off the cliff. For men, this is the last aspect to develop. Men jump and if they land safely, they tend to run off to the next thing. Slowing a man's "jump" could be significant in knowing if he is worth keeping. Food for thought?

Men desperately feel the need to be nurtured and admired. Conversely, men are not instinctively nurturing. Men are very caring, loving and protective but often express it in ways which make it difficult to recognize, and even can be interpreted as controlling. Sometimes they *are* controlling, and it's hard to tell the difference. Any memory of this confusion will linger. In a relationship, men need to be able to understand the needs of others, without thinking about it, but rather to sense it. This is a very difficult task for men, especially when those things are far down on their list of "important things to do." It is often said men want to be mothered. I am not sure that is far from the truth. While not really mothered, men do appreciate being guided by their partner and give in freely on what they consider mundane. A man only wants to know when, where, what time, and how should he dress when it comes to everyday matters. Men are simple, but comfortable, and choose not to deal with the emotional side of what they consider to be a woman's world. This is one reason men often have difficulty understanding a woman's emotional viewpoint and don't feel things at all like a women. Many things they turn over to a woman, often mistakenly, are things they feel are unimportant. Given that men so easily lose sight of the importance of things they don't want to do, (i.e. housekeeping, picking up, childcare), it is no wonder that they end up viewing the female's huge effort as less important. This has a large negative affect upon the relationship, and promotes the idea of a lack of care and understanding for what the other does and what they do to make things work.

What Am I Thinking?

Women yearn for the connection that binds a couple and for their man to instinctively know their needs and wants. This is a learned behavior for men, and since they must learn by asking, making mistakes, and trying to do what pleases their female partner, this becomes a very awkward and clumsy effort, which seems to fail men repeatedly. This is perhaps why women have unmet expectations in relationships. What they expect from a man is beyond his nature except as learned behavior. This is not what women want, but men at least spend considerable effort and time trying to make their partner happy, trying to meet the demands, trying to be romantic, emotional, and connected, although it's generally a guess. With men, failure isn't from lack of effort; there is often considerable effort made in erratic directions.

Women also make huge efforts to express caring and love toward men. Cards, notes, poems, gifts, special dinners, or gestures all are a part of showing true care. Those efforts often leave a woman angry because her man doesn't respond as desired. The man is usually confused by those gestures and doesn't verbally reinforce appreciation. Things which do work with men are usually sexually oriented, or boy toys, or things the women can do with little change in their basic personality. Men are so very predictable that it's not hard to please them. Many women seem to think they shouldn't have to express care in ways other than exactly how they wish. Yet, most women feel very comfortable asking men to show care in ways that are alien to the nature of men. Men do appreciate a woman's efforts. They often just don't show appreciation in the way a woman feels is complimentary. Effort, even halfhearted, is still effort and appreciated by the man, unless it is used like a club, a reminder of how much was given. This seems to be a pattern in relationships which have slipped or are in decline. Both sides continue to be willing to show appreciation but want to keep count of who does what for whom. If one or the other partners in the relationship begins to keep count, it is a sign that a search for a reason to leave has been initiated.

Connection matters more than anything after the initial attraction brings people together. For the unknowing, (read men), liking someone is helpful; it at least provides a road map for some of the issues confronting men in trying to show moments of spontaneity and romantic thought. The connection is what makes a man want to spend time with a woman and to invest himself emotionally in her. It's important for a woman, it's important for a man, and most important, for the couple to succeed, primarily because of the nature of the differences between us.

Jeremiah J. Jordan

Absolutes

Things you must have.

VS

Things you can't stand.

What must you have in your next partner? Make a list. Be honest. No, I mean *really* honest about what you must have and can't stand. You might surprise yourself. You might find you're a bit shallow, closed-minded, or more emotionally damaged than one would like to admit.

What will the partner bring to your life?

What is the benefit for you?

These are questions we ponder when we join a dating site or the dating services from the old days. These questions are popular to ask because people *absolutely* want to compartmentalize others so as to only have to make choices about what they think they want. We have a built-in set of biases as well as additional ones we develop from relationship failure, life learning, and just maturing. All of us want to have it all sorted down to one or two we can pick from with at least some certainty we are headed in the right direction. It may work that way if people told the truth, or if our perception was the same as theirs. The difference in how people see themselves and how they are seen by others is often huge. We all have looked at people when we are out and ask ourselves *"Did they look in a mirror?"* It's just fine in this world to be unique and to still want to find someone who will love you. Just remember, the further we place ourselves from the mainstream, the fewer choices we have.

Viewing absolutes—the things we can't stand—often touches upon many things we would like to think we have overcome or gotten past. It takes some really deep searching of ourselves to be able to recognize if we have truly moved on. We probably need to ask ourselves why we picked some of the absolutes we must have in a relationship. There are many absolutes—both the *can't stands* and the *must haves*—which may define us more than we truly wish to be but are significant to us if we ever wish to find a partner. What, exactly, are absolutes, you might ask? Absolutes can be:

religion	handicap	height
education	weight	children
income	intelligence	race
vehicle	body type	ethnicity
weight	profession	smoking
drinking	culture	fishing
sports	hair	language

And there are many more, some we don't even realize we have until we run into it them. Most of us can't imagine we are so narrow-minded until we think about it. Oddly, when we are in the selection process, we don't seem to ask the right questions to get the right answers regarding our absolutes. Here are some examples of the "right" questions we should be asking. What answers are you searching for . . . really?

Can I depend on him?

Will he steal from me?

Will he hurt me physically?

Will he lie to me? (real lies . . . not little white lies)

Will he stop caring for himself?

What will he be like after the new wears off?

Does he give up when life knocks him down or does he keep going?

Will I be better off with him than without him?

Absolutes can influence our selection process to the point of excluding good potential partners. Consider some concepts we have touched on earlier and overlay your absolutes on them.

- o   Men are at fifty what they were at eighteen unless impacted by an external change event, generally a negative one.

- o   Males you wouldn't ever have considered dating when you were young because they were boring, or nerdy or not cool exhibited the behaviors then which you want in a man now.

- o   Being judged by appearance doesn't matter unless you don't think you look good.

- o   I will never be hurt like that again.

It seems we don't often think about our absolutes until we notice how annoying our partner is. We end up negotiating with ourselves about the things we can put up with—and knowing inside we really can't. The outcomes of these situations are as predictable as they are common: unhappiness, separation, or the slow, agonizing, mind-numbing relationship status of being with someone you no longer want. I think that staying is far worse than leaving, but our culture and socialization doesn't allow for a straight forward approach. Even when we spent time considering the absolutes, we often tend to only pick the superficial ones, such as looks or money—the things which are not enduring. Sometimes, we feel we can be "OK" with a thing or learn to live with it. Many times, especially for a woman, some have the idea that a partner will change and be different. They won't. If he is not what you want right now, he will never be. Most women know that; they just hope it's not true for them. One of the saddest things I ever heard was a beautiful young women crying about how her boyfriend treated her, saying, "I want to be the one there when he becomes the man I know he can be." Are there any thoughts on what happened with that relationship? Was her patience and pain rewarded by his awareness, personal growth, and development? Did he become the man she saw in him? The survey says . . . NO!!!!!!

Often we find it impossible to compromise with ourselves, even when we should. When we are young we believe we must refuse to settle for less than we want. When we mature, we refuse to settle again. Perhaps, if there was a better idea about what is really needed to be happy, there would be better outcomes. It is hard to get where you want to go if you don't know where you're going but we seem all too happy to repeatedly run in the dark. Our rigidness and pride keep us from having a better chance of finding someone who will love us—and that we can love in return.

As you think about the absolutes in others, also think about how you present yourself. We often forget this is a two-way process and likely the other person is as bull-headed and unrealistic as you. If you don't like who you are, it's likely someone else won't either.

Men don't look into a mirror with clear or critical eyes; they view the world through a testosterone filter. Yeah, the stuff that makes them stupid most of the time. Most poor decisions men make are testosterone related. That includes relationships, cultural errors, criminal behavior, and accidents involving automobiles, guns or bars. Knowing this, a woman can understand why men may show interest yet be of little interest to her. Smile, enjoy the attention, and go on. The woman, however, should be clear. If she finds all the men showing her attention to be less attractive than she desires or thinks she deserves, she may need to re-evaluate her own presentation. Since men are very consistent, their actions can be used as monitors or benchmarks for women to assess their marketing presentation. This can be extremely useful in developing more realistic expectations when designing a marketing plan, in understanding to whom she is marketing, and what her target audience is thinking about her.

Both men and women can come to the conclusion that they can't have what they want and that level of acceptance is usually reached in anger. It would be helpful if we could at least admit the problem is with us and accept that it's stubbornness that keeps us alone, not the problems of those that don't want to be with us. People who make statements like "*Well, if they leave they don't deserve me,*" will likely have very few others in agreement. Most times people in our circle of acquaintances or co-workers can see very easily why someone is alone; they just don't want to rock the boat by saying so.

Jeremiah J. Jordan

Sex

Once upon a time, (pun intended), a man and a woman married and they had no knowledge of sex prior to their wedding. Historically, we don't know when this time was but it might be reflective of what we think Victorian England was like. The experience was new to both and, since they were young, any contact of a sexual nature was wonderful and mysterious; all was agreeable with the couple, as far as sex went. The first time down the path is still a wonderful journey if one has nothing with which to compare.

Reflectively, many consider that first trip clumsy and, for women, perhaps painful and somewhat demeaning. Men, fearful of their limitations, realize that if a woman ever figured out she might be missing something, that sex, circumstances, or life could be better somewhere else, that someone or some other man would treat her better, be more caring, gentler, or be a better lover, there would be discontent. This discontent would lead to insurrection and lack of control. I have known for years that women knew that and could utilize that knowledge to their advantage yet have not done so. It begs the question, *why?* Some man at some point realized that if he can train a woman to feel guilty about sex, then he can keep her connected to him. Its remarkable how we teach women and how "The One" concept influences them in a sexual way. The concept that loving someone makes sex better is pounded into adolescent boys and girls. Boys, and then men, tend to promote this concept and use the "love" word more as a means of seduction than an expression of feelings. It is amazing how many women, who after years of marriage, when separated or divorced and experience their first "other" sexual experience, can't believe what they were missing. Sexual pleasure has a lot to do with being with a good lover and very little to do with loving the person you are with. Being in love can add to the connectedness, the warmth of cuddling, but almost nothing toward the sexual quality. This further complicates the dating process for adults as we are more aware and wary than we were when first in the romantic process. It is important to understand what we have experienced, and what we came away with. Did we like how we were treated? Did we enjoy or did we feel lessened by what happened? Whatever happened—good or bad—influences every choice we make going forward.

We have entered a period where safe sex is not only important, but critical and that sharing sexual history has significance. It is important in being able to understand the impact of our sharing. Men often struggle in completely sharing the numerical extent of their sexual activity. You will most likely get the complete history, as far as sexual actions, from a man: what they have done and, to what extent, with whom. A lot of men are serial monogamists, each time entering into a relationship hoping for the best and to build a lasting connection. For such men, while genuine and unintended, the number of sexual encounters can grow to a high degree over the course of many years; however, as far as emotional impact, only one or two may have stood out as significant. Other than the health issue, asking good questions and coming to know what made those few relationships significant would be helpful in understanding the man. Men like to discuss all things sexual and women need to feel comfortable having these conversations with a man in order to learn more about him. Questions concerning the *types* of sexual acts can provide information about his likes and dislikes, but not an accurate number of experiences. And, since men are not often good at expressing connectedness and affection verbally, a woman can use her power of language and emotion to explore why he felt connected to a former lover. A woman should not feel uncomfortable exploring these issues to learn more about the man to whom she is attracted and connected. She should remember that the significance of the responses never was about the sex but the feelings toward the person which made those questions important.

For both men and women, just numbers can be confusing and often unimportant. It is important to discuss activity and events and to work toward sexual security. A common mistake to avoid: Never, ever tell a man you did a sexual act with a former lover that you are unwilling to do with him. You might as well just get dressed and leave. You can either not say it, unless there is a medical reason, or agree to enjoy it with your new lover. Remember, men need to believe they are all that there is . . . it's a male to male competition, and if the man thinks you did more with another man, he will always believe you loved the other more. Intellectually we know this has nothing to do with love or even emotion but we still need to understand how information affects others and how to best work with that knowledge.

There is a belief that when a woman has sex with a man soon after meeting or quickly into dating, this somehow hastens the departure by a man due to her being seen as "easy." This idea is not only false it has created additional problems for the dating process since sex is so greatly tied to dating. At some point there has to be some level of acceptance by women that sex will neither make a man stay nor cause him to leave. It really doesn't matter if it's a first date, the first fifteen minutes of the first date, or the twentieth date. Great sex can cause a man to stay a little longer and bad sex can cause him to leave a bit sooner. The preservation of virtue, so to speak, has virtually no effect on a man's decision but it does serve to allow a woman to make better choices and learn more. It just should be understood, whatever the choice, it will have no noticeable impact upon outcome. Men don't care. If a man is attracted to you and likes you he will stay; if he does not he will go. Men want to have sex no matter which scenario is played out. The man has more than likely decided if the woman is relationship material or just a sexual partner. Her behavior sexually has little impact upon his notion or desire. Understanding this can be of great help to the woman in making decisions regarding sexuality and relationship selection as well as reduce frustration.

As grownups we have been there, done that, know what we like and don't like. We have expectations. For men, often it's to just orgasm. For women, it seems to be everything besides orgasm. Well, that really isn't fair; most women express they want an active sex life. Sex is a big part of a grown-up relationship. Women seem to have a different perspective about what is an active sex life. I am not sure that women are wrong because their perspective involves connection, intimacy as well as sexuality, and these are the things that have an ongoing connection in the relationship in which her flirtation, sexuality, and physical displays of affection are an expression of her affection, connection, and love.

To men, women appear very complex. I am sure women can express similar sentiments regarding men. I believe this occurs because of our distinct differences in how we view the world. Men see a thing and want to fix it; women see the same thing and want to make sure everyone feels good about it. All men had a mother, and often, what "Mom" taught us lingers, especially how she cared for us. Mom also gave us narratives about what to think of other's behavior that we continue to carry as well. That is probably why men seem to want to be married to three women: a mother, a princess, and a call girl. In an effort to meet their preconceived needs and wants, men act is if they need one woman to take care of them, one to take out into public, and one for the bedroom. This would come close to meeting men's different perspectives of life. As most women can attest, it is unlikely one man could keep one woman content, let alone three. Men do like compartmentalization. This is not to say men are right in their desire or wrong because they want it, but this may shed some light on some of the disconnected thoughts men seem to have about what relationship life should be and how to make a woman feel loved.

It is important that both partners are content with the sex in the relationship. The frequency of relations, specific sexual acts, and verbal communication before, during, and after all need to be what each in the relationship feels good about. If one or both partners are not satisfied with the sexual situation, it creates incredible strain on the relationship at the most crucial point where trust is maintained. It really doesn't matter what the sexual desire of the couple is as long as both partners are content with it, comfortable with the outcome, and secure in not losing their partner's love. Swinging couples, voyeur couples, non-sexual couples, men married to prostitutes or exotic dancers, cross dressers, bi-sexual partners, no matter what the particular proclivity, anything, and I really mean *anything*, is acceptable as long as it's agreeable with both of the partners. The sexuality of a relationship is the glue which helps the relationship as a whole endure good times and bad. Sexuality has a huge impact upon the trust level between the couple. The intimacy involved with the physical act and the vulnerability which exists all become connected to the larger relationship picture. That is why it doesn't matter what the sexual preferences are, just that both parties are equally content with it. Without the trust that comes from that mutual contentment, it is impossible to maintain an emotional balance within the relationship and between the couple. When that balance is disrupted, since trust is involved, there is a loss of ability to communicate. The subsequent disconnection can affect not only sexuality but also the acceptable level of attraction. The damage may impact the connection with the partner and absolutes can change.

The importance of these four components to a relationship's survival is generally connected to the idea that relationships are never fifty-fifty. If one of the two in the relationship is not satisfied with attraction, connection, absolutes, or sex of their partner, the relationship will eventually fail. If the missing component(s) cannot be restored to the point of satisfaction, the relationship will end. That doesn't mean there will be a divorce. It doesn't mean that there will even be a split. It does it means that the reasons the relationship was created are gone and if the couple is still together it is for different reasons. Will people stay together for the kids? Will people stay together out of duty? Will people stay for the money or security or fear? Of course they will—and make excuses all along the way. And when one of the components fails, we are back to the three options already presented and the ongoing impact they have on potential happiness.

Chapter 5

The Scale

When people leave us, it is because we have failed to meet one or more of the Four Components of an Adult Relationship. It may be no fault of ours or completely of our making. It will always fall to Attraction, Connection, Absolutes, and Sex to define if a relationship will exist, how long it will last, and how much happiness we will share.

Jeremiah J. Jordan, 2011

For women, there seems to be a universal agreement that men should have more substance to them, at least a bit more substance than is usually observed. Women would like men to be more expressive of their feelings and for them to have the ability, without being prompted, to openly show their feelings as well as being more warm and emotional. It would be nice if their men could and would talk about their feelings and open up to their female partner. That sounds like a reasonable expectation, and most men would do this, were it not for the fact that they would have to participate in such unfamiliar territory. And, there is that little thing about a man's feelings needing to coincide with what women want to hear. Many a man has long known that if what he has to express isn't what the woman in his life wants to hear, he is better off to just say something else or, perhaps, nothing at all.

The more I know about men . . . the more I like my dog . . .

It is very true that it would be quite comforting for women to know men could be different, and to be different not only in how they view women, but how they make choices about women and relationships. Women would like men to make relationship decisions based upon a woman's inner qualities and personality, not the woman's physical package. Some women don't mind being a "physical package" and for them it's perfectly fine how men choose a woman. Maybe it just depends upon the package. Women have long suspected men's heads are turned by a pretty face, a smile, large breasts, long legs, flesh, sparkle, and pretty much anything that reminds them of sex. Women could not be more correct. An occasional annoyance, perhaps, but this isn't really a bad thing. It doesn't make men pigs, or sexist, or scumbags or evil, but it does make them the half of the species that ensures survival. It's not conscious, nor planned, it just is. Men are very predictable regarding females; this carries over to who they want to date and with whom they want to have relationships. This concept is not actually quantifiable to any degree of accuracy. It is, for lack of better understanding, locked into their genes as well as their jeans.

From listening to the rhetoric, it seems women generally believe that men should be different. That difference is predicated on the idea that if men were different, it would be more likely that a woman's hopes and expectations could be fulfilled. It appears at times that women need men to be different so as to justify the romantic belief system that repeatedly fails them. It seems that there is almost a desperate need to believe in the hope that they can vindicate themselves for making bad choices. It's like a woman thinks *"When I find the one it will be worth the wait and pain I have endured over the years at the hands of selfish, lying men."*

Perhaps this is too simplified an analysis, but one that is not entirely without merit. Both men and women tend to paint an entire gender with the brush they got from their last heartbreak. Once we reach that point where most of our life is behind us, we are carrying a lot of grief around regarding past choices and decisions. Unfortunately for most of us, the opposite sex is the only real direction we can go with the feelings of loneliness we wish to resolve. It is sad to so often hear such negative perceptions of reality, especially those making categorizing statements that make connecting more difficult. My mom told me Santa Clause, the Easter Bunny and Superman weren't real; I took her at her word. I can tell you with all sincerity that men who are portrayed in romantic comedy and romance novels don't really exist.

Keeping the faith can be difficult and an investment of decades waiting for "Him" and the dedicated belief that "He" is there, somewhere, makes for a weary existence. "The One" that women so want to exist—perhaps only to justify the years of disappointment—at the very least interferes with and at most prevents making the best of current opportunities and situations. It can cause them to miss real chances to be happy, and they often hold onto that hope believing their "One" is out there, just out of sight and out of reach. All of us want to believe things magic, in mystery and that we will be happy when our "One" finally comes to us. It would be cool if pigs could fly, but I won't hold my breath waiting for it to happen.

A Graphic Analysis of the Situation

For a woman to understand how men go about the dating/mating selection process they must take a slight step sideways. By that I mean, for a woman to understand how men view women and to make decisions about who to approach, women must step away from their usual perspectives. This is probably a far longer (and maybe larger) step than is comfortable. For men, searching is not emotional or even with thoughtful consideration toward the future; it is numerical. While it makes sense to them and their male friends, it does not make any sense to most women. This is due to the difference in how the world is viewed depending upon which sex is doing the looking. For men it is numerical in the sense their choices can be quantified and scaled or even graphed. Numerical also, because men are being genetically drawn to procreate, instinctively knowing the greater the number of partners the greater the likelihood of offspring. Men unconsciously are open to a larger pool of possibilities. There is little to no emotion in the initial selection process. It's a lot like point and click.

Unless pressed, men just wander through life directed towards women and a relationship based upon drive—but not reason. If an acquaintance develops between a man and a woman to whom he is attracted, there is a lingering aspect for the man where, if he could have sex with her, he would. The idea of "Friends First" never enters into the man's mind. As touched on earlier and put as plainly as possible, a man only dates women he views as potential partners for sex. The term "date" is used very loosely here. I think men would prefer not to date at all. They don't mind the going out; it's the ritual of vying for approval which is frustrating to them. Men don't like that the choice of sexual behavior isn't left up to them. As far as selections, men will voluntarily only talk to women they view as potential sex partners. So women, if a man just opens a conversation, for no apparent reason, you are in his "YES" group.

There are exceptions for work, and colleagues can become fond acquaintances without the attraction. Men also will talk to anyone when they need help or when they have to. Generally, women do very much the same. To a woman, what point is there in spending time with someone they can't see themselves being with unless there is an external motivation outside the likelihood of a romantic connection? Men will have many conversations with people they don't find desirable; it is usually because they are in the person's line, need to get past them, or are being polite. It is not because that person is someone the man wants to get to know. At first glance, there seems to be a significant difference between men and women due to a sliding scale men appear to have in their heads. This refers to the unpredictability of who is and who isn't desirable to them. Conventional thinking was that no such scale existed for women, but after further review, the idea likely needs to be revaluated.

None of this is to say men and women can't be friendly or caring familiars, or close acquaintances. It is possible for men to develop friendships with women. This is usually when sexual interest is not a part of the mix. In other words, the man isn't attracted and looks past that to listen. As much as women would like it to be the opposite, it isn't. Please ladies, take two deep breaths, swallow hard and don't throw rocks at the messenger. It does no good to get angry at me for something that over and over is proven to be true. And again realize, just because you want a thing to change for your benefit, doesn't mean it can change or even should change.

This non-attraction "friend" bonding experience also changes the dynamic of time spent together between the man and women. It's never going to be a date in the man's mind. Going Dutch or pay your way is expected, humor and observation of other women is expressed with the idea the accompanying female should just endure it. The female isn't perceived as a potential sexual partner. This also tends to make the male act like he does with his male friends by not treating her as he would a woman in the "would have sex with" group. This is as close as a female will get to the male version of friend. However, depending upon the length of time since the last encounter or amount of chemicals in his system, the man may enter into sexual behavior with the woman, in a "this means nothing but need orgasm" situation. In his mind, she has the correct equipment, she is available, he is . . . well, you get it.

Making Choices . . .

Men commonly view a large number of women as potential sexual partners, but only very few of that group as desirable for a relationship. Let's take, for example, that a man views sixty out of one-hundred random women as potential sex partners—that is saying he views them as reasonably attractive. In the man's mind that is a wide field of possibilities for sex. However, of those sixty, only fifteen he considers having a relationship with. The other forty-five he would have sex with, without blinking, but consider them as unacceptable candidates for a relationship. To understand this, we have to understand how men chose sexual partners. Men don't see with their eyes the whole woman, the complete package—the inner and outer total woman. It is as simple as a singular physical feature, a dress, a pair of shoes, or a smile. A woman's hair, eyes, figure, anything can attract a man toward a sexual encounter. Liking or hating the woman has no impact upon her inclusion in the group of potential sex partners. Rarely is there any initial thought to relationship or marriage or even what happens after sex. A woman either is or isn't in the group. No pondering or reflection or deep thought occurs. There are some situations which can change that and even expand the inclusion group. Alcohol definitely has an impact as well as how long since the last sexual encounter. Sufficient amounts of either can lead to expansion of the group to nearly 100%. Men have different preferences when it comes to women. Men have different tastes, they like different things. This means all women are included by someone. Refer to the "15 Minute Rule."

That doesn't mean all women are included in the relationship pool. This is an important point to consider for women. It is relatively easy to get oneself excluded from a man's relationship pool. Once a woman is downgraded or exclude from the potential relationship pool, it becomes for the man a negotiation with himself. How much time, effort, and money is he willing to commit until reaching his goal? The woman's elimination from the "relationship" group changed the dynamic and redirected the goal of dating, the updated goal being specifically . . . sex.

With genuine sentiment, women are often confused when men advertise to be what a woman wants because they have forgotten why men date. They are then surprised when a man turns out to be other than how he has presented himself. This old Chinese proverb says it best: "*Fool me once shame on you . . . fool me twice, shame on me.*" I don't blame a woman for being upset about being lied to; however, if a woman fails to accept the reality of why men date, they are eternally doomed to repeat being misled. Women often clearly state they want X. Men want women to like them. Men can say they are X or whatever they think a woman wants to hear. Men intend for women to believe they are in the relationship pool when they ask them out. To women seeking a relationship, men are not going to say they are not interested in a relationship. Otherwise this makes achieving the primary goal much more difficult. That is why men rarely say *"I want to take you out for sex,"* or *"You're really cute, what do I need to do to have sex with you?"* Actually, men have tried these tactics and for most men that level of honesty never works. So, as far as getting their half of "needs being met," men have learned how to adapt to other methods.

We have to take a moment and consider when a woman forces a man into a mold he doesn't fit into, even an imaginary one; the man will likely follow his nature. Generally, a promise is sincere when made, often forgotten when pressed to live up to it. The regret that follows is genuine and not for the action itself, as the man feels little or no regret for this, but rather for feeling vulnerable to a woman. Nothing excuses men from objectively lying or misleading a woman for sex. This is a decidedly un-chivalrous act and should never be tolerated. However, out-and-out lying is not the same as the previously discussed "little white lie" which is considerably different and driven by the instinctual desire to procreate which always trumps the desire to resist.

As long as women insist upon holding to their position regarding what men's intentions should be and they continue to rail against the reality of male dating motivations, discussions regarding males expressing their dating intentions honestly cannot work. There is the possible exception of when money is involved. Men clearly understand that concept. That situation isn't what dating for adults is about but makes a significant point as to the unlikelihood of actual disclosure of intention. Men are very simple beings. Men really try to avoid complications; they want things easy and predictable. Consider the four components of an adult relationship: attraction, connection, absolutes and sex. Knowing "what women say, and what men hear" explains a lot about failing dates, unmet expectations, and ending up alone. Just because a man views a woman as a potential sex partner doesn't mean he will like her, that she meets his absolutes, or that there is sexual compatibility. It means, based upon his observation, he would have sex with the women—period. Understanding this and accepting this will be greatly beneficial to women as they seek a partner. Knowing men—instead of hating them for what others did in the past—is a step toward finding a successful relationship.

While it may seem odd to women, men will have sex with a woman they can't stand only because they are attracted to them. This illustrates the gaping difference between men and women in how they view one another, dating and sex. Women say that they feel they need to like a guy before they can have sex with him and some women say they must have feelings or love for a man before they can have sex with him. I have often wondered if that connection difference or emotion is in any way connected to the physical aspect of our sexuality. With men having external sexual organs while a woman's are internal presents some additional things to bring to the mix. Hosting another person inside one's body is considerably different than penetrating one. It is an entirely different dynamic. It makes sense and also equates to the driving ego men have about being chosen. It's not just sexual drive, it's egotistically driven, competitive, and at the core of instinctive male behavior. It was also pointed out to me that for a woman, pregnancy consumes a year of her life while the man is virtually unaffected. The instinct of that would likely drive a greater desire for selectivity in the female. The ability to control conception has greatly affected that aspect but instinctively, it likely is still deeply ingrained into decision making.

I swear to tell the truth, the whole truth . . . maybe

It is true that men are often no more than pond scum when they lie, but how much has that lying has been influenced by truth not working for them? While impossible to say for sure, we know omission can still be a lie. At the beginning of dating, intent may be genuine and the initial attention sincere, but after further review of the female and her personality, interest wanes. It's like you're cute, you're boring, and I still want to have sex with you, for now. The biggest flaw in men's approach still is to have sex knowing there is no intention of relationship and misleading a woman. And the struggle which confronts men is, if they tell the truth, how do they resolve the ongoing balancing act between biological pressure and intellectual resistance? There is no excuse in either gender pretending a relationship exists and verbalizing it with no intention of actually having one. Whether for sex or security or entertainment, no reason should allow one person to intentionally mislead another using emotion as a tool.

As a rule, men usually prefer not to care about a woman's personality or inner beauty unless she is also potential relationship material. In many cases, at least for men, no talking is a good thing as it gets in the way of the goal. Most women have figured out if a man won't talk with her, she is not being viewed as relationship material. So, no matter what inner substance a woman has, it is unlikely the man will pay attention to it or even listen well enough to find out unless they happen to be in a very narrow "potential relationship" group. The man will feign romance; say what the woman wants to hear in hopes of finding the right *combination to allow for sex. Cologne, dressing up, cars, dinner, phone calls, gifts, candy, and* flowers, whatever works to achieve the goal. If it often seems the guy is quickly going all out throwing everything into the mix, it is because he is. The search for the key is obsessive and becomes more important than what to do with it once you get it.

That obsession can be seen in an often used phrase "Candy is dandy but liquor is quicker." I don't know who said it but it has been a tried and true method of gaining favor since alcohol was discovered. While not a moral compass it does a good job in representing a purely male outlook toward women not considered having relationship potential. Is it morally wrong? At times it would seem so and at times not so simple to know. Unless one is breaking the law or lying about it, it's probably not morally wrong. I mean, adults can choose how much they drink and should understand potential outcomes. The thought that "a man wouldn't do that with a woman he cares about" is a misguided and empty one. Look at how many boyfriends have gotten their girlfriend drunk for that very reason. Bringing up these points is intended to highlight that obsessive behavior. The drive toward the goal is so powerful to cause significant behavioral changes in men. The idea that men will be different or can be, or want to be is a fruitless pursuit. Understanding likely behavior is much more useful than hoping for another's good behavior and not getting it.

Some things which may help clarify men's outlook on dating, women, and sex are:

- Men can have sex with a woman they find attractive and have no desire to build a relationship.

- Men can have sex out of curiosity.

- Men can have sex to relieve stress.

- Men can have sex because they are relaxed

- Men can have sex to solve problem

- Men can have sex after a fight

- Men can have sex to celebrate

- Men can have sex because they are sad

- Men can have sex because they are bored

- Men can have sex because it's a day ending in <u>Y</u>

- A man's thoughts on a date go no further than the first sex event. A woman thinks about the things coming after the event. Men and women have conflicting expectations with regard to why each is there on the date.

Men—By the Numbers

The following graph tries to illustrate how men view woman and how they select them for various aspects of interaction. As the graph shows, there is a clear distinction between YES and NO. A YES means that the women is assigned to one of the working or interactional Sub-Groups. NO means they are excluded and not considered for any interaction beyond necessity. Men are not really confused about this. To be clear, YES means a man will view a woman as a potential sexual partner on physical attributes alone. This critical decision is made without conversation, with no history, no idea of who or what the woman is about or her qualities beyond the strictly physical. As far as the NO, the same means of measurement is applied. The decision is quick and generally final. A great personality will have no influence upon this grouping. Inner beauty has no effect upon where the line is drawn; this is totally about attraction. This is the first piece of the puzzle that is the male selection process.

The numbers used in the graph have no meaning other than to make graphic the groupings. They don't reflect any actual numerical values.

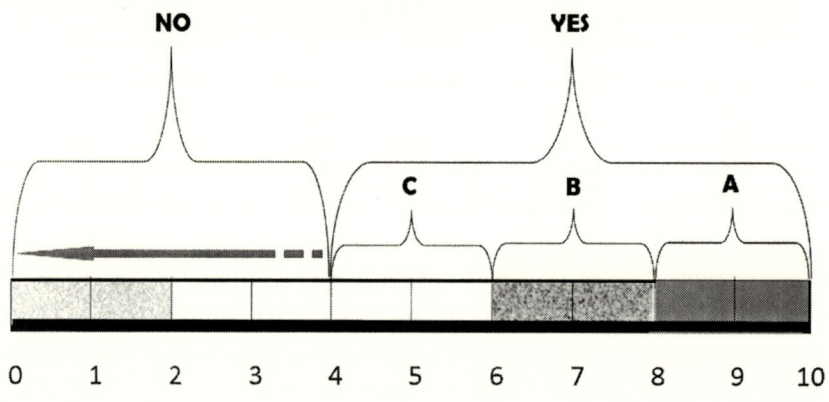

Figure 1

Sub-Group A: Beyond Reach

In Figure 1, there are three Sub-Groups to the scale all falling under YES: A, B and C. Sub-Group A is a group comprised of women that the man feels are beyond his grasp or out of his league. The thought is that sex would be great but unlikely unless she was on drugs, drunk, or the man is rich. If the man is rich, this group still exists but likely there would be different women in this group. Men believe any type of relationship would be impossible with women in this group because the man doesn't have enough substance, money or looks to keep them. Additionally, women here are believed to be *Extremely High Maintenance* due to the level of attention their attractiveness has garnered them. Honestly, most men never look at themselves realistically, so this is a pretty small group. But all things are relative. Nearly all men have those women they consider out of reach. This group can change, adding and deleting prospects as life changes and as the man moves up and down the socio-economic ladder. It appears that men fall a bit short on the character scale by using this evaluation process for women. Since the unattainable, high maintenance woman appears to be driven by money (and most often this is the case with a "Gold Digger"), many men perceive the price tag as too much to afford. Window shopping is still an option, though.

Whether through jealously or shaky self-esteem issues, men tend to think money has a lot to do with the choices women make about men. True or not, there seems to be as much conviction on the part of men that money is the driving force of female selection as women's conviction that men choose based upon physical attributes. This is a continuing theme for men and is part of their flawed process of selection. Additionally, there are some generalizations about women having money being spent on them and whether that is an "investment" for a man. To clarify, this is not a negative but it is a behavior that occurs in the dating world. As a vehicle of conversation, dating can be considered as primarily entertainment. If a woman goes out with a man and enjoys an evening with no intention of pursuing a relationship or meeting the man's desire for sex—and doesn't tell the man ahead of time—is that any less deceitful than the man who takes out a woman with no intention of a relationship just for sex?

As far as I'm concerned, this is clearly six-of-one and half-a-dozen-of-the-other. And yet, a man taking a woman out just for sex is almost universally denounced by women and male bashing becomes the acceptable behavior *du jour*. The other is covered with *"He asked me out and shouldn't expect anything in return."* Obviously, this seems unfair and totally out of place. I agree with the later, but disagree with the former with equal fervor. A woman can't be hypocritical about these two behaviors and expect not to create conflict when trying to find a male partner. Men can live on one side or the other of the issue; women have to be philosophical and pick a side—then live with it. As Grandma always said, *"What's good for the goose is good for gander."* That would, however, require a decision which is final and not subject to changing at whim or due to inconvenience. Ladies, make up your collective minds and make a definitive choice about what you want—a "friend" or the possibility of a meaningful relationship—bedroom games and all.

Sub-Group B: Relationship

Sub-Group B, the second part of the scale, represents the women that a man feels are relationship suitable. This is not a large group. In the man's mind, this is a very select group. It is unlikely that the man can identify why these women are in the group or what qualities they possess. He may also be embarrassed to admit the true reason he chose them. These are the women, at first sight, that the man can see himself with years down the road (but he sees her down the road looking exactly as she does now). To men, the aging process is not constant, consistent, or realistic. This is a very important group to understand because, for the man to have a relationship, the woman must be in this grouping. In the man's mind, these women are the combination of attributes they have come to want in their partner. These are women who meet the attraction requirement, and again, this is attraction alone. As humans, we have no control over to whom we are attracted. Within this group, are there women to whom the man can see himself connected? His mind is almost instantly filled with images of his favorite things with her as a part of them. A man can spend countless hours thinking about a woman he has never met and fitting her into every aspect of his life. This isn't an infrequent behavior and is pretty normal for all humans. It just seems odd for men to think and fantasize this way, given their pragmatic and objective behavior.

Being removed from the sub-group is as easy as gaining entrance. It is a very fluid group based entirely upon whim. Since the category is based on attraction only, the other things which make up a person are most generally excluded or considered as givens. Being dropped from the list is as mysterious as being selected for the list due to lack of reasoning for how a woman got there in the first place. It is usually a very short trip out of the group with nearly anything being sufficient cause. This is where the nature of the person comes in to play. Remember, in the man's mind, a woman assigned to this group is often thought of as near perfection. Since only physical attributes are considered, no real person can fair well under scrutiny. Nagging, annoying voice, personal quirks, phase of the moon or that he saw something more interesting all can mean early exit. The lesson in all this is not that men are idiots. They may be, but men are not going to change how they look at women. The real lesson for a woman is that getting angry because of what a man sees as attractive and expressing it toward men in general is not only futile but hurts her effort to find a relationship. Men don't want to be around a woman who bashes their gender, especially for something they can't help and have no motivation to change.

Men seem to make most relationship decisions based upon a simple formula:

$$attraction - perceive\ negatives = X$$

It is a simple formula. Only the man knows what X means or what the passing score is. He probably can't define it but the feeling drives the man either into or away from a relationship. There is a subtle difference between men and women in this regard. Let's say, for the purpose of example, a woman begins with a score of eighty in the man's mind; she can only go down from there, never up. Some women who start with an eighty can actually do such things as to make her drop her totally out of the potential sex partner group. During a date, a woman can make herself completely unattractive and undesirable, as can a man. Generally speaking, however, a woman stays where she is in a man's mind unless she does something to cause a negative reaction.

Sometimes the man will put up with a lot and keep the woman in the Potential Relationship Sub-Group. If he gets caught up in "The One" fantasy, he likely will put up with additional issues and rationalize to keep the women there. You noticed I've said *rationalize* and not *resolve*. Humans, as wonderful as they are, are not particularly suitable for tinkering but then there is that nagging fantasy of "The One." It can easily be manifested in an appearance, history, family, geography, or any singular aspect of the person. We are what we are. How often have men married a woman because she was packaged the right way and wrapped much more beautiful than the essence inside? While not exclusive to men, men don't usually believe they can change the women, they just believe it won't matter. Women, on the other hand, exclusively make up the group which views their relationship partner as a project.

It is rare if a man elevates a woman from his initial perception because of a positive act or behavior. There are many things which can drop a woman from the Relationship Sub-Group to the Sex Only Sub-Group and there are not many things that can elevate one. Food maybe, breast enhancement possibly, but I can't think of any others. There are aspects in a woman that make them more appealing and attractive and can influence an upward movement, rare, a statistical anomaly certainly, but it can happen. Remember, men are very simple. Just because women are complicated, doesn't mean that men have to be. In a long term relationship, marketing isn't important but if you're back in the dating pool, it is critical. It is foolhardy for women to spend energy being mad because a man doesn't appreciate how wonderful their personality is as it gets them no closer to a relationship. It does often convince the man to drop the women from the Relationship Sub-Group.

The second component to adult relationships, *Connection*, or liking an individual, cannot elevate someone into a different sub-group. However, this is where the aspect of connection can be critical as it keeps a person in the Relationship Sub-Group. There are times during dating, where there may be some short term "relationship" behavior, but the influence of the Four Components of a relationship, as discussed earlier, will eventually win out. That is why it is so common to see adult relationships last one to six months. They often start with both parties having great intentions. Attraction, connection, absolutes, and sex are all working but as time and knowledge increase, absolutes begin to show up, communication becomes more labored and sex becomes less satisfying.

As far as falling from the sub-group, things that can cause a man or woman to be removed from the "relationship" sub-group would be anything that caused one not to be liked by the other. This is a pretty broad category, but it works for both genders. Most of us have experienced a moment when talking with someone we may think attractive or even special in some way, when their entire demeanor changes—like a switch. We know something happened; often we ask them and they give either no response or a casual, *"Oh, nothing."* What happened in that moment is that we felt a message, a message that we just fell out of their "relationship" group. And it's over. It may take years to die, but it's over.

If a woman believes the man only wants sex, then she has some indication as to which group she has been assigned. With this knowledge, she can smile and be flattered, or she can become indignant. If the guy is nice she can choose to go out or not go out and this is all up to her. If the man realizes he won't get sex within what he feels is sufficient time, he will go away. By accepting the man as he is, a woman chooses the direction and outcome of dating. There is no harm in going out with a man only interested in sex as long as the woman gets the final say. The only negative thing involved is the woman being angry at the man for being himself and her refusing to have a life because men are not what she thinks they should be.

There is considerable truth that a friendship can make for a great relationship; it also can make for a wonderful partnership even without the attraction component. However, in that case, it will always be something other than a complete relationship. For most of us, a nearly complete relationship would be much better than some of the ones we have experienced. There is always hope in the possibility of making a connection or a friendship into something more. Attraction can be fostered with some personal adjustment. Many of us have seen the stories and movies about the "Ugly Duckling." A plain woman has a makeover and is beautiful. A perfect guy falls in love with her before the make over and then is rewarded for loving her for her inner beauty. Sometimes he doesn't realize he loves her until after the makeover occurs. I love this story, and would like to believe I could be that man. I think most men, knowing their desire to be noble, like the concept. Reality, however, makes for a much different action, behavior, and outcome. The "lead a horse to water" analogy is appropriate here. As humans, we just can't feel something. If we don't feel it, we don't feel it. We can't like green if we don't like green. We can tolerate it, put up with it, rationalize about it, and endure it but we can't want a thing that we don't want.

Sub-Group C: Sex Only

This is the group that gets men into significant trouble. It is where the most horrible things said about men can be traced. As briefly stated previously, alcohol consumption or time without sex can greatly affect behavior. The downward limits of the "Sex Only Sub-group" are flexible. "Women get better looking at closing time" is a popular saying. Alcohol is a social lubricant and often a sexual starter. Men and woman under the influence will say afterward *"Oh, My God!"* realizing who they had sex with. Since we all know the outcome of drinking, this behavior can't be a surprise. It is an excuse for behavior—some wanted, some wanted less.

Women in Sub-Group C are often very attractive, marginally attractive or not attractive at all to most men. It is totally in the eye of the beholder. It can be as simple as how she looks in a red dress. It can be as complex as a beauty queen with a horrible personality. It is simply the Sex Only Sub-Group. This is a large group and it increases every day. Once there, it's difficult to be removed. Since the man has no intention of having a relationship with the woman, there is little cost for continued inclusion. Circumstances such as commitment, engagement, marriage, being mean, a bitch, evil or even alien (from another planet alien) do not remove a woman from the Sub-Group. Death, yeah, well that might do it, but little else. Yes, men will have sex with a memory. Why do you think men go back to reunions hoping for a chance with the cheerleader who wouldn't talk to them while in school? If she said *yes* now, in his mind it would be with the memory of her back when he first knew her. How men select woman to date and how they do the mental gymnastics regarding females, past and present, is directly related to the fear of vulnerability they hide from the world. It is those conflicting aspects of the male that makes understanding men, their choices and their erratic dating behavior even more confusing for women.

Additional to this is a frustrating conflict men have when they are attracted to a woman. Men realize that attraction makes them vulnerable to a woman. We have seen it over and over how men are not only tempted but, while knowing better, succumb to that situation. Men are pretty good at being faithful when no woman is paying attention to them. Men are good at being faithful when a woman they are attracted to is paying them attention and their relationship, work, and self-esteem are in good order. If a man is attracted to a woman, and his relationship, work, and self-esteem are in crisis, the more attention an attractive woman pays him the more difficult it is for him to remain steadfast. Being weak to any woman with whom a man is attracted is not a circumstance men wish to be in and it is uncomfortable to them. We have seen many men sell the farm, so to speak, during these times. Women additionally deal with similar issues, generally attempting to resolve the same needs as men. While we think there is a vast difference between the genders, our behaviors tell us different stories.

Women—By the Numbers

While it may be offending to a woman to know that men use this rigid yet unconscious selection process, it is safe to say that a woman's selection process shares many similarities. There is a built in quick, YES or NO for woman as well. Women openly deny it, but after a brief conversation with them, they will start making their choices apparent. There is a division between who a woman goes out with and who she will view as a potential sexual partner. So, women also have a Potential Relationship Sub-Group. Men would view the Entertainment Only Sub-Group as being placed in either the "friend zone" group (dreaded and feared by men), or the "I will date you, spend time with you, let you spend money on me but will not sleep with you" zone. This is part of the total confusion process for men. As clearly established, men don't ask a woman out who they don't view as a potential sexual partner. Men become confused when a woman says "yes" to a date invitation; she gladly goes out, yet doesn't consider him "that way."

I would say as women become more mature, they seem to draw a clearer line between "dating men" and "relationship men." Most likely they have learned about poor emotional investments, or involvement with "friend zone" men. There seems to be a pretty distinct and predictable selection models for both genders, so it is hard for one sex to throw rocks at the other. We still throw rocks but we need to accept that we are hypocritical when we do so. We can't really expect others to be different if we are unwilling to change. This issue of disconnect is critical in understanding men's and women's disappointments in dating. The disconnection is a failure to have one's expectations met as well as not understanding the other person's motivations and perspective. It's not being able to adjust to the situation. So we crash. That being said, men know becoming intimate is the woman's choice. Men would prefer that women, who don't view them as at least potential sex partners, just say 'No, thank you" and not waste both of their time or his resources in an unfruitful pursuit. Women don't say this for the same reason men don't tell women they only want sex. It is another little white lie but this time by the female. Declaring an absolute "no way" to a man would take considerable power and potential entertainment options away. If a man is positive the women won't ever have sex with him, how often will the man ask her out on a date?

Earlier we mentioned a deeper look to consider that women use a similar method or scale in their selection process. The following graph tries to illustrate women's view of men and how they select them for various aspects of interaction.

The numbers used in the graph have no meaning other than to make graphic the groupings. They don't reflect any actual numerical values.

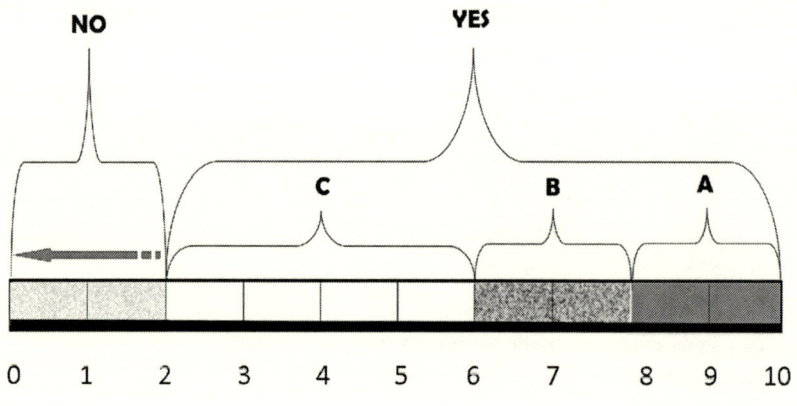

Figure 2

As with the male graph, there is a clear distinction between YES and NO. Women are not really confused about this and seem to understand this process between themselves, but it is quite confusing for men. Strangely, the Storybook effect continues to bear poisoned fruit even here: the idea of a woman seeing what no one else can see or the desire to be present when he finally becomes "the man he can be." We have seen this often, especially when women are in adolescence, and the choices they make. The 1980's band, Goldfinger, says it well in their song, "Is She Really Going Out With Him?"

Friends First

Is she really going out with him?

Is she really going to take him home tonight?

Is she really going out with him?

Cause if my eyes don't deceive me

There is something wrong around here

Around here.

Pleeeeeeeeeeeese . . . hit me in the head with a rock . . . .

To be clear, YES means the woman will view the man as a potential entertainment partner on physical attributes alone, without conversation, with no history, no idea of who or what the man is about or his qualities beyond the strictly physical. The group is much larger than the man's due primarily to what men consider the Friend Zone grouping. Women can have a larger selection because they don't intend to ever have sex with anyone not at the far right of their scale. As for the NO side, while for men a woman can rarely fall from right all the way to left, for women that journey can be quickly made by perceived personality or character deficits. Men would have sex with a serial killer they find attractive; women will drop a man to the NO group, as in NO CONTACT, because of a red flag, a sensation of character defect, a lingering "something isn't right" (female intuition) or just knowledge of behavior the woman sees as not to her liking. For women, the decision is much less quick and not nearly as final as with men. A great personality will have influence upon this grouping. Inner beauty has a positive effect upon where the line is drawn; this is much more inclusive of the whole person than the male scale. It is, as with the men's, initially based upon attraction but is flexible as to upward mobility for men on the scale. This is the first piece of the puzzle that is the female selection process.

Sub-Group A: Beyond Reach

In Figure 2, there are three Sub-Groups to the scale all falling under the YES heading: A, B and C. Much like the men's, the women's Sub-Group A is a group comprised of men that the woman feels are beyond her grasp or out of her league. Women often have a "would do" list as in *"I would do them"* (sexually). Not a real list of men to have sex with but if George Clooney or Brad Pitt offered, a woman would trip them and beat them to the floor so he would land on top of her. The thought is that sex would be great but unlikely, so it's a safe list, just in case a miracle were to happen. It is a different perspective from that of the man's Sub-Group A list, but reaches the same outcome. If the woman is having sex with George Clooney or Brad Pitt, then the list will adjust to other, out of reach, men. Women never truly consider a relationship with this group—well, maybe non-psychotic women—but allow for imaginative sexual fantasy.

Sub-Group B: Relationship

The second in the scale, Sub-Group B, are men the woman believes are relationship-suitable. This is not a large group. As with men, women consider this a very select group. This would be the group considered a "catch," so to speak. While a woman initially picks this man by attraction, that alone won't keep him there. As with men, there is a composition of qualities the woman wants and she either realizes he doesn't have them or rationalizes that he will once she is done with him. This reminds me of the woman who yells at her husband of twenty years as she cries saying, *"You're not the man I married."* This is true since she began trying to change him right after the ceremony.

Unlike men, women can often speak quite clearly about exactly what qualities, perceived qualities, or desired qualities the man has that brings him to this Sub-Group. She is generally very proud of those, either real, imagined, or planned. Women often use the term, "to grow old with" which is converse to men's concept as they never want or really consider that their woman will age. These are men who, at first sight, "Wow" the women's senses. These men also, at first communication, bring a sense of what the woman wants in a man as well as indicators of less than desirable qualities, although she may not, initially, heed these warning signs because of the "Wow" factor.

Often in Storybook type stories or romantic comedies, men and women are at odds at the beginning of the story but they come to fall in love through interaction. As cute as this is in fiction, after adolescence it isn't what often happens. As women become adults, if they have been through a relationship or two, it is likely that red flags will go up regarding a long list of issues. Men, who exhibit any of them even to the smallest degree, are immediately excluded from further consideration. Women will, to a certain degree, give points for personality but a minimal attraction must exist. It is very important to understand this group, because for a woman as with a man, to have a relationship the man must be in this grouping. We should remind ourselves once again, as people, we have no control over with whom we are attracted.

Sub-Group C: Entertainment Only

This is the group that angers men, but which women feel most comfortable. It is the "Friend Zone," to use a man's description. Women will go out with these men, allow money to be spent on them, and have no sex, nor do they feel the stress of having to contend with sexual situations. Regardless of their attraction level, women put into this group men with whom they can feel safe, feel no sexual pressure, no sexual attraction, and no desire to be with beyond hanging out. Friends with benefits (FWB) often can fall into this group. However, the woman either is more into the guy than she admits, or it works only for a short time as the woman will upgrade quickly to a man with whom she sees as more likely being in her Relationship Sub-group. Upgrading in this manner isn't difficult for the woman; generally, a simple *"Do you want to?"* would suffice to close the deal.

The nature of the "Friend Zone" can at times involve errant sex, usually limited to one or two times. The guy often is in love or fascinated with the woman; he thinks it's real, but the woman regrets it and feels the encounter was a mistake. As briefly stated previously, alcohol consumption or time without sex can greatly affect behavior and interactions with individuals in the group. For men, the downward limits of the Sex Only Sub-Group are flexible. For a woman, alcohol can contribute to men in the Entertainment Sub-Group becoming sexual partners. Additionally, as with men, chemicals and length of time since a last sexual encounter can have a tremendous effect upon where the lines are drawn.

Male vs. Female Selection Comparison

What do the two scales have in common?

1. Both Scales have an identified "out of reach" zone

2. Both men and women identify a narrow grouping in what they consider their relationship zone, and this is probably-based upon "The One" concept. The narrow gap of "relationship potential candidates" are slightly different in that females often set higher expectations but settle for lower outcomes while men sent lower expectations but don't settle below the initial standard.

3. Both scales slide left with alcohol or time without intimacy

4. Both scales have a grouping which is exclusionary as far as contact, other than work.

How are the scales different?

1. Women give points for personality, character, sensitivity but men don't. Women take points away for lack of same and men don't.

2. For men, once a woman is on the YES side, it is unlikely she will be removed. This is due to inclusion on the YES side and is based upon the determination that she is a potential sex partner. For women, men can easily and quickly be thrown to the NO side.

3. The area to the left of the zone for men is the sexual area; the area to left for women is for friendship/entertainment.

Friends First

The pyramid below represents the scale groups put together

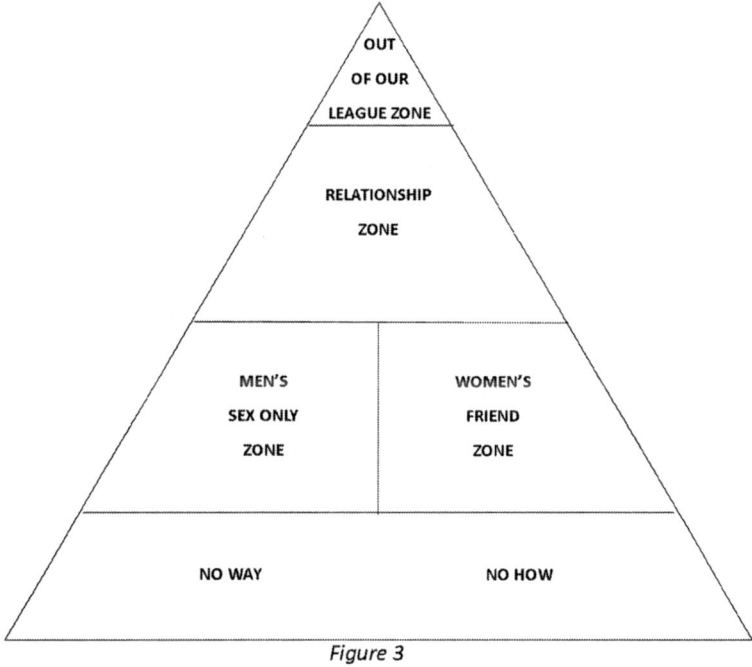

Figure 3

Men and women have groupings that are not only similar, but nearly identical as far as division and order of grouping. Again, as stated in the introduction, no empirical research was conducted, only anecdotal. But think about it: we can always debate the size of the groups but we must realize they do exist. We know from our experiences, from conversations with others, and from our own interactions that they exist. Women don't consider themselves as being as numerical as men, yet both sexes fall into similar mating selection patterns. These patterns have developed over time and promote the behaviors which help our species to survive. We have a clear methodology for pairing that we follow. Technology and industrialization have allowed for more people to interact but do we interact differently. More people mean more choices and, therefore, more bad choices. From tribes to the internet, a vast difference in the number of contacts exists but little difference in human behavior and motivation occurs. Like *Romeo and Juliet* and *Harry Met Sally*, great tragedies as well as great comedies have sprung from romantic encounters which were misconceived, at best.

It is easy in a world of no choices to have no temptation, but as humans, that curiosity is what drives us to be more than we are. Control is comfortable but it's not human friendly. We are often in a constant struggle with social concepts and learning experiences from childhood and education which conflict with our biological and emotional processes. Because of our life experiences, our ongoing attempts to control our offspring's mating decisions and behaviors most often fail, just as our parents' attempts to control ours usually failed. As our world became more and more diverse and complex, paths took us away from cultural expectations which were more duty than emotional. We were unprepared for the number of options which opened up to us and unable to adequately sort through them to make correct choices. Our failure to save ourselves from ourselves and our bio-emotional drives often resulted in a poor choice of a partner. We unfortunately have to learn new methods of dealing with the sheer number of options and how to evaluate them for our best chance of success.

In a world of only apples, one is not much different than another. In a world of a hundred fruits, or a thousand, or ten thousand, choices expand; the issue is more complex when picking the one to eat for the rest of your life, and for that to be the only thing you will ever eat, no matter how badly it tastes. We may have dreamed of a great apple and for a while it was great, but we didn't know what an orange tasted like. It is easy to say we are people not apples, but our behavior toward a thing tells us a lot about how we perceive everything. Our personality and instincts are not selective; they are connected to every part of us. Our satisfaction or dissatisfaction tends to grow with time. When our simple expectations are met we are happy and if they are not, it influences or re-directs our choices. If we enter a situation with excitement and expectations are not met, it erodes everything in the relationship. And, in a world where partnership doesn't mean survival, where the complications of modern life present emotional conflicts we are not well prepared for, it is predictable that relationships are more fluid. It is no surprise that more and more grown-ups find themselves again searching for a connection. Life spans have more than doubled; yes, we have the same set of instincts. We hope and dream and live on faith that "The One" is there, even when our experiences tell us a different story.

Chapter 6

Hope?

*The best way to never get hurt is to never try. A favorite quote **"a ship in port is safe, but that's not what ships are built for." Grace Hopper** so eloquently says that we can be safe, but at what cost? In our security, we pass by opportunities and the clock ticks away. We are alone.*

Jeremiah J. Jordan, 2011

This book was never intended to be overly critical of either men or women. In some ways it is pretty hard on both and presents a dark outlook on the potential for either to overcome their natures and find happiness. They are two deeply entrenched opposites refusing to budge; one from genetic inability, the other out of emotional demand. Both are seeing themselves in the right and waiting for the other to change, both making efforts to compromise yet with effort not sufficient enough to move the rock that is the human ego. I have not imagined that in this book are words adequate enough to change a species' direction and behavior. It is my hope that I have been able to describe some behaviors and ideas that will help us move forward more successfully by learning more about one another.

The goal of this book has always been to point out our problems and to stimulate thought. It has been directed primarily toward women because within them is the potential for adaptation and success for both genders. It is my hope that by knowing men better and understanding how a woman's efforts can affect men negatively, women can utilize that information to be more successful in finding a relationship that offers them a higher level of satisfaction. I am sure there is some frustration at the thought of making an effort while men seem to not have to change. I would perhaps smile at women and remind them that someone has to go first so the group can succeed. Additionally, I believe that a first-step effort can lead to a more open exchange between men and women which, if anything, will reduce pain and hopefully allow for more successful relationships to occur.

I hold out little hope for men to change, evolve, or become more aware. In our social development, the ongoing emasculation of men over the past fifty years and neutralization of male-like qualities, except in movies and athletes, will continue to erode men's ability to responsibly connect with women. Without a clear role, instinct will further drive behavior. I believe it may take several generations for clearer roles to be defined. How a man was once defined to himself and others is lost, and what they are to be now is still undefined and contrary to genetic programming. Men carry with them a lot of confusion and some anger, not really knowing why. Women have made substantial gains in redefining their roles. Most of us see this as a positive with both professional and social progress being made. Men are confused about their place in it all because it has changed. This is a good time to bring understanding and acceptance to the discussion instead of anger and intolerance toward a thing that is instinctive and not learned. If a woman wants a relationship, she has to stop communicating in a way that makes men not want to have a relationship with her. A man's Relationship Sub-Group is small enough to begin with and there is no need to make it smaller due to a contrary attitude or stubbornness.

All said and done, there seems to be a pretty good case for never becoming involved in a relationship, or at least many reasons why we shouldn't. We have looked at how women react to men and build walls to keep relationships at bay. We have examined men's failings and how women view them through either rose-colored glassed or the lenses of contempt and discontent. Any sane person's first reaction may understandably be *"What's the use?"* Most of us felt that way at one time or another. Our response is usually swearing to never try again. But as humans, we are driven to couple, even when we don't want to. Men will easily flow back into pursuit of women, but only after building walls to protect themselves from becoming emotionally involved. Men don't see a conflict in dating for sex without the possibility of a relationship. Women often are more timid about relationships and have difficulty trusting. Since women have differing goals in dating, it can make it harder for them to even make their presence known in the dating market. Timidity and shyness are not rewarded with attention. The impact of past experiences makes it harder for both men and women to move on, to be able to trust or even try. Think back to a time when it has happened and you likely can still feel the weight of the experience upon you.

As for women, if they can come to the conclusion that men won't change, that men are what they are, and accept that, there is hope and progress that can be made. If men can see women as they are, different in perspective and level of emotion, there has been some headway made. If there is effort toward acceptance, then there are some positive outcomes available. For men to do this, they have to be with a woman who understands male motivations as not evil intent but just a part of being a man. This will allow for more useful communication instead of the usual building of walls and rock throwing.

I don't truly believe men are going to change in how they approach dating or how they view women. Men have a long list of frustrations about women which are all but forgotten with a smile, or touch on the arm, or even a "hello" from a woman they find attractive. When men are in love or are infatuated, most men know which of the two of the couple is in charge. Men gladly give way to split roles because it gives them comfort and predictability. Mixed roles which occur more and more often are confusing, cause strain, and often have varying degrees of success. As most things between couples, it depends upon the couple how successful the relationship will be. Women shouldn't change who they are for anyone; however, a different methodology for women may be the answer to move toward greater relationship success. Not a change in values or beliefs, but acceptance of how men are and using marketing strategies which maximizes the potential for positive outcomes. That point may seem somewhat overstated, yet I think the first three or four times it is heard by women, it is summarily dismissed and forgotten. Repetition here is designed to allow for a broader look at what is a critical aspect to the problem.

If the biggest obstacle to a woman finding a partner is her ability to accept that men are the way they are, that also gives an indication of the first step in being prepared to date. Women say all the time *"Men are what they are and don't change."* Women know this about men. They express exactly how men are, often saying it in an observing way instead of with anger. Women laugh about men and men's behaviors, but in their heart they seem to believe—or at least hope—that Prince Charming is going to walk up to them or at least answer their profile. So it's all there—the "Keys to the Kingdom"—and still women don't accept or realize how to work with the knowledge to their benefit. Because a man views women initially in a sexual way, his outlook means very little toward developing a relationship. Forgotten in all this conflict of wills is that sex and all sexual behavior is still the women's choice. No matter what, sex is up to the woman.

I know what is going through your minds now; *"I just won't have sex with him until I know he is "The One."* Isn't that what you're doing right now? It is important to note that not having sex will only keep a man interested in direct proportion to his level of expectation of the pleasure of the act with the women in question. It is a cost benefit analysis. Men will allow, either consciously or unconsciously, most women three dates to close the deal. This is to determine how much investment a man wants to make in a woman before calling it "good." This includes the Relationship Sub-Group as well as the Sex Only Sub-Group. If a woman is in the Relationship Sub-Group there is more latitude in extending the "sex" deadline. Perhaps until commitment or marriage, this is often seen as the female's goal, depending upon a man's attraction for a woman and how well she can keep him interested. The idea of sex will keep him interested for a while. This is a variable due to maturity and how well the man knows the ins and outs of dating. Having sex on the first, third, or fifteenth date will have no effect on a potential relationship but may put an end to dating sooner. Perhaps thinking of men, sex, and relationships in a different way will help.

If a man is going to stay, sex won't end the relationship unless it's bad sex. Again we have to consider the impact of the last of the Components to an Adult Relationship, the impact of sexuality on the relationship, and the need for there to be sexual parity. If a man is going to leave, sex won't keep him around unless it's great. Men compartmentalize sex and relationships; they aren't the same thing and often have only minimal impact upon the other. It is understandable how frustrating it is for women not to know into which sub-group the man has placed them. This is similarly frustrating for men if they are in a woman's Friendship or Relationship Sub-Group and neither gender shares each other's insight, as it defeats their progress toward their respective goals. Perhaps we need to be asking more insightful questions of one another.

If we meet someone with whom we have an interest, outcomes will not be positively influence by residual fears, emotional baggage, or the rigid denial of the obvious. Just because one doesn't want something to be a certain way rarely determines how it truly is. Also, if we don't allow for a thing to be what it truly is, we will later have to deal with the backlash. Forgetting or ignoring that all things will return to their nature can be a painful thing. A useful and often quoted illustration of this is the story of *The Scorpion of the Frog*.

The Scorpion and the Frog *is a <u>fable</u> about a <u>scorpion</u> asking a <u>frog</u> to carry him across a river. The frog is afraid of being stung during the trip, but the scorpion argues that if it stung the frog, the frog would sink and the scorpion would drown. The frog agrees and begins carrying the scorpion, but midway* *across the river the scorpion does indeed sting the frog, dooming them both. When asked why, the scorpion points out that this is its nature. The fable is used to illustrate the position that the behavior of some creatures is irrepressible, no matter how they are treated and no matter what the consequences. (The origin and author are unknown; Wikipedia, 2011)*

It is always better to understand, accept, anticipate, and enjoy rather than to ignorantly believe and be unhappily mired in the situation. It is ever worse to imagine, mistakenly, that the situation is managed and controlled, when it is not. Fear is a huge motivator to us and as a species it makes us do foolish things. We will openly accept harmful options. *A drowning man will grasp for the point of a spear.* We will try to build walls to keep that which we fear away. Even when we don't know what we are fearful of, we build and reinforce and hope. We are delusional in our belief that by limiting ourselves we can limit the potential for bad outcomes. While we cannot completely stop bad outcomes, especially when we make bad choices, that same action can limit the opportunity for positive outcomes. Limiting ourselves by putting up walls is a blanket approach. It is indiscriminate. Just as in the rest of life for increased security and safety, we have to give up something. Fences and gates, even the emotional ones we construct, affect everyone, not just those for whom they were built. To protect ourselves from emotional pain we equally limit our ability for emotional joy. As with real walls, trying to see over them or through them limits our ability to see clearly and understand what is on the other side. This translates into not being able to clearly see one another. Since the goals of men and women are similar but the paths are so different, it is helpful to know how the other makes decisions. It is also helpful and rewarding to measure everyone else according to what they bring to your life, how they can add to it and enhance it, and not in accordance with what someone else did.

Perceptions are Reality

If you spend any time looking at any type of dating process—online, printed personals, or anything where there is a profile with a list of "requirements"—you will find an overwhelming abundance of contributions by women who so limit themselves with their requirements that no mortal man can expect to fit into the mold. Here is an example (paraphrased from actual profile):

> *Seeking attractive, tall, Christian man who enjoys long walks, outdoors, children, and family. Must have stable work; be financially secure and romantic in nature.*

That doesn't sound too bad on the surface except for what men take from it, what it isn't saying but is still required. This type of profile is asking for a guarantee of a blissful fit with no chance of pain. This man doesn't exist in a grown-up, single format. Well, there are the men in a Storybook romance novel, the operative word here is *novel*. He could be a widower, but that won't last long, and locals, searching for a robust opportunity, will likely snap him up before he ever hits the open market. Or, he could be a never-been-married or secretly relationship-phobic guy who just needs a little "fixin'" to make him "all-better" due to any lingering damage the last woman did to him many years ago, possibly in high school. Maybe God will provide.

When we forget who we are marketing to, we lose track of how to market for success. After that first broken relationship, everyone is tainted, flawed, and carrying way too much baggage. A much better approach with a real chance for success would be:

> *Wanted: Man attractive to me who would enjoy getting to know a thoughtful, attractive single mother. Outdoors or indoors are both fun. I work and am active and seem to fit best with similar men.*

Wow! That's too simple. We often forget the simple premise that, as a person, "I cannot find a way to be happy if my expectations are unrealistic." It is a good thing to set personal goals high and slightly out of what we think to be our reach. We still can't control others, only ourselves. In the realm of finding a partner, we must always look to expand the pool of prospective interests and only be exclusionary about things which are absolutes to us, not just things that will protect us from being hurt.

In the minds of men, women like to tease and flirt. Women like attention on their own terms, but say they are looking for the right guy as if it is a "Get Out of Situation Free Card!" Like many men view women, a woman's intent is variable depending upon what man is with her and into what sub-group the man falls. Wow! . . . just like a guy.

Women express that men don't want to date, are too shallow, or just plain strange. Men believe that the puzzle that is a woman is not worth trying to assemble because when you give them what they say they want, they don't want it or it isn't enough. Women express the belief that men will never realize that they don't want to be used as a one night stands or just for sex. Men do realize that, but also have to deal with erratic behavior which sends mixed messages and inconsistent reactions where a woman walks away from a good partner to be used by a bad one. Men often feel that there is no point in respecting a woman's wishes since women don't seem to respect their own wishes.

Women feel that the romantic part of a relationship needs to come first and that a man demonstrates love, care, and commitment prior to intimacy. Men want to be sure of what they are getting and that there isn't an empty promise lurking. Women do their fair share of pre-commitment marketing which seems to fall by the wayside after the commitment. While men can demonstrate love, care, and random romantic acts, men don't feel those things in an ongoing manner. Generally, men only are romantic to gain favor and would prefer if women understood that and the whole romantic thing could be put aside. Women want a man to show a prolonged expression of want, need, and desire to be connected. Men want women to take their word for it (not a good idea) and, depending upon how they view the woman and what Sub-Group she is in, men will continue to demonstrate a corresponding level of commitment. All of a man's sweet and cute romantic acts will fall quickly away as they were marketing tools generated intellectually to pursue a goal, not acts generated spontaneously by feelings. Women have a "doomed to fail" belief system that tells them a guy can always be romantic. Women expect that men should feel spontaneously romantic because women do. Women believe that the romance should never end, and that an ongoing and endless emotional honeymoon should occur normally for a man. Men feel an initial rush of infatuation, and are driven to pursue it through all known efforts to gain favor. Again, there is not a real connection to these acts and the emotional state of the man. Consider it logically: When buying a big ticket item, you've paid for it once. Does it make sense to keep making payments? For a man, romance is a part of courtship, to win favor, to earn the right, to be called upon, to be bestowed the reward. It is not an ongoing function. A man may deeply love a woman and yet have zero "inspired" thoughts about romantic acts. Because he cares he will deliver them, thoroughly thought out, researched and, above all, learned, but *not* emotionally inspired.

Women who have been hurt while dating often pick up on the concept of no sex on the first date as a means of self-security. Understanding the social management concepts we teach our children and how they follow us along to adulthood makes this an easy decision. Most men accept this as a cost of dating, rather like a cost of doing business—marketing the product. Since all aspects of relationships involving the physical are in the hands of women, the man's focus is on impressing the woman to gain favor. The choices are not the man's. Some women prefer the "no first date sex standard" thinking that most guys just disappear anyway, so why should she waste time and good sex on a loser? To be clear, I am not advocating that a woman should or shouldn't have first date sex; I *am* saying that as far as an impact upon a potential relationship goes, it makes no difference in the outcome.

Men often view female attention as just teasing, wanting a free meal, or attention without actually acknowledging, let alone, addressing the man's needs. Men feel they far too easily become the bashing board for women's past relationship mistakes. I believe men do take more than their fair share of bashing from women. I also am sure women become the object of a man's wrath to an equal extent as both men and women tend to take out our past pain on others.

Women may or may not understand that men can't tell the difference between flirtation and just being nice. While wedding and engagement rings clearly denote a category of "spoken for" women with boyfriends need to wear something to let men know they are taken. While we know that won't happen for many reasons, we do know women are flattered when men pay them attention and they have the ability to use the *"I am seeing someone"* line as an exit strategy. While not an assurance that a man won't continue to flirt with a woman, married, engaged or attached, seeing a symbol gives notice that the exit strategy is readily available. *Proceed at your own risk.* Men completely understand this and are not bothered by it. Men resent flirtation and then dismissal and it reinforces in them lack of trust in women and their tendencies to mislead and misinform. It is a chicken or the egg problem, and we tend to pass it on to our friends. It does none of us any good.

Most men are not very good at reading the subtle clues, the messages women send like *"I like you-ask me out"* or *"I would like a kiss."* For men, we need to know what you mean because otherwise we will get it wrong, not intentionally, but still wrong. For men, the physical is simple: it is or isn't, and men have been wrong too often about dating, so it's easier not to ask. There isn't a speed built into men for "a little." Men don't have a mode for a little kissing, a little affection, a little hugging. So, when the man goes along with small kisses and harmless not-so-close-relative-like hugs, to them it's not the beginning of an exploration of the joys of mutual affection or the heightening of desire through delayed gratification. It's like having a meal put in front of them that they can only smell. That doesn't make the meal taste better; it only makes a guy frustrated and angry at the one withholding the desired objective. I have yet to find a valid study showing that delayed gratification is any more satisfying than immediate. What I am sure of is that with delayed gratification, we tend to dismiss it quickly because it doesn't meet expectations built up over time.

Since men are unsure of what a female wants, what her alluding to affection means or what she wants him to do, a man finds himself in the same scope of behavior that has worked in the past. Often on a date, when a woman wants to hold hands or softly kiss, men already want to be intimate so it's easily interpreted as a green light. Women are so fearful and attuned to men taking advantage of them, so it really doesn't matter what he does; he will either be too physical or not physical enough.

Men rarely think of a woman as a one night stand, but usually think they are in the YES group. The one night experience is generally a result of what happens that night. If it's a great night, the man will want to again; if it was an average night, and the woman isn't in the Relationship Sub-Group, it will be a one night stand. There are a few truly one night situations and both sides should be aware of the nature of the interaction.

Honesty

Let's accept, as a given, we all prefer honesty to lying. In women's profiles they speak often of finding an honest man. We know this is the intersection of opposite goals and that men believe if they are honest and don't play games with women they get screwed, and not in a good way. Men believe that if they tell the truth so the woman knows their feelings, it not only leaves the man vulnerable but it will not result in a positive outcome for him. How do men know this? They have all tried it and it turned out badly.

Boys, and later, men, do try honesty but are not rewarded for it, and as a matter of fact, are admonished for it and treated like they are horrible people. Let's not forget who does the admonishing and then initiates that poor treatment. That is not to say the girl or woman should have rewarded the behavior, but when a person gets no reward for a behavior, that has a neutral effect which can lead to seeking a behavior which will provide greater reward. When boys/men learn the truth doesn't work (usually a very harsh lesson from a girl/woman) they also learn a white lie forwards the effort toward the goal. So what action do you think they chose in the future?

Unfortunately, the white lie becomes bigger and ever increasing as to succeed with a more competitive and untrusting female group. The man believes he must go through this process because if he is honest, women outside the relationship zone would likely not have sex with him, which is pretty much true. Since he is not rewarded for honesty, he will do what works; so many times it becomes comfortable behavior. This process is inevitable, primarily because men are instinctively driven to it and there is no evolutionary motivation to change. Women don't flock to men with honesty traits so as to pass on those genes with more frequency. Women control sex. They control who they are with and what happens. They are passing on to future generations of women exactly what they wish for them to have as partners.

Women frequently say that they want honesty. Oddly, when they get it, they often reject it saying, *"You shouldn't feel that way."* If I had a dollar for every time I have been told my feelings were wrong by a woman, I could afford to take out women who know better. From most men's perspective, women spend way too much time telling them how they should feel, but that is another book. The rejection of honesty appears to be because it's not what women want to hear. This is very confusing for men. Remember, men are simple. Imagine the poor guy wanting to please the woman. He is struggling with *"If I tell her the truth she will get angry and I have no chance to get what I want."* If I tell her what she wants to hear, well you know how it goes. Men cannot change the basic truths of why they are with a woman. Neither do they want to nor can women force them to change. The angry reaction only convinces men to be less than totally honest. Women seem frozen in the position that they would prefer to try to change the wind rather than fix the sail.

This has to change if women wish to be successful in relationship building. This is not to say that women should give in and let men do as they wish. It means by accepting the reality of why men are there, their motivations and their nature, it eliminates the need for a lie and therefore communication can be dedicated to exploring the possibility of a relationship. If you know he is motivated for sex, know he isn't romantic and your short term goal is to determine which sub-group you have been assigned, he can be encouraged to be himself, and you can see if you want him.

A man does what he has learned to do to make a woman happy. It doesn't come naturally. It is learned and, often through trial and error, sometimes learned badly and sometimes learned very well. Romance is not something men just think of or do naturally but when motivated men can be very romantic. To be clear, no matter how badly women want it to be different, no matter how the hero behaved in the romantic novel or the romantic comedy, men aren't that way. It isn't comfortable or what women want to hear; men are romantic because they want sex, not because it's natural for them. Men are romantic because women want romance and men do what women want in hopes of gaining favor which translates into sex. Women don't want to be thought of as objects for sex, and this is fair enough. But if the only reason men ask them out is because they consider them potential sexual partners, where does that leave us. The sooner there is acceptance by women that it is that drive for sex that motivates a man to ask them out, the sooner women will have the opportunity to see if a relationship is possible. Accepting, at least in principal, would be a huge advancement in understanding and awareness about men and what makes them go from point A to point B. Instead, women likely will continue to want men to be different than they are and complain they want more of what a man doesn't want to do anyway. During the quest for the prize, men go to great lengths to express romance, and perhaps women should appreciate men's efforts more, so when the romantic façade goes away, it isn't a big surprise. We know that won't happen, but an understanding that the drive for the goal, not a romantic nature, fostered the desired behavior.

There are times while infatuated, men get goofy and they often do things which women feel are sweet and endearing. Men tend to get over this quite quickly. Adolescent boys are taught about girls/females primarily from mothers, aunts, sisters, school mates, advertising, music and movies. All of them talk about the positives of flowers, cards, gifts, random acts, and sweet things to impress a girl. Boys listen and do it and see positive results. Boys do what works. Boys abandon what doesn't. This is human nature. Boys figure out a smiling happy girl is more likely to kiss than an unhappy one. Kissing leads to . . . more.

Players, Head Games and Objects

Women often use the label "players" to describe men who go out with women for sex and run away. The label indicates that the sole purpose for asking out women is sex and that lying and manipulation are the trademarks of that kind of man. Often when describing what they want in a man, women clearly state they don't want players or liars. Who would? That seems to be a "goes without saying" type of thing. Men who actually fit those descriptions are few, and while it may not seem so, represent a very small percentage of the whole of dating men.

Women point out frequently that there are many men who play head games with women or intentionally mess with their head. Simply and directly stated, for men, women are not a game. Men have a goal, and they pursue it. The only issue is into which sub-group the woman falls. The term *head games* must be intended, by women, to explain that men show interest and it waivers or expresses initial interest that quickly fades and that there is a conscious process to keep a woman dangling and not moving forward or back. There is rarely any attempt to mess with anyone's head. What may occur is if the woman is in the YES zone, men are prompted toward their goal and depending upon circumstance and past history, will modify their tactics again depending upon her sub-grouping. If she is in the Sex Only Sub-Group, the man may like her, enjoy the sex but has no intent in a relationship beyond what has already taken place. He is not motivated to end it if he still is getting the desired outcome. I am not sure any of us, men or women, are motivated to end anything from which we are getting the desired outcome at minimal cost—are you?

From a male perspective there is a vast difference between viewing a woman as a sexual object and viewing them as a sexual possibility. A sex object would seem by definition to have no other function. Again we go back to having to know into which sub-group the man has placed the woman. Generally men don't limit what things a woman can become to them, or what role a woman takes in his life, as long as she is in the relationship grouping.

Sleeping with the Enemy

Neither men nor women wanted to reach this point. For those who found their partner young, married that person and continue to be happy, *kudos*, you are a small minority, a statistical anomaly, but good for you. Now be quiet, because you create an unrealistic expectation for the rest of us who's original dream already died. Ones who married their high school sweetheart and stayed married until death-do-you-part avoided the pitfalls of post break-up relationships. The rest of us who have endured the death of The Dream would have liked to have had that life. We have to deal with the reality of what is and stop moaning and grieving about what has been. We can either make that choice to move forward or continue to do those things which prevent us from having a chance at a successful relationship. The more complex our social structure, the fewer and fewer "ideal" relationships exist and, in all likelihood, are probably fewer than we realize or want to imagine. When we add in open marriage, playing around and the like, that number may be very low.

The result is men and women can be distrusting of one another, with each wanting something the other usually can't provide. Men want open and unrestricted access to sex with desirable females. Women want romance, caring, and to be made to feel special and loved without the complexity of sex interfering but know that at the right time, at their choosing, her man will be a torrent of unleashed passion unto her and her alone. Women reject men's honesty hoping that a man will come along and will act as they wish him to act. That might happen at seventeen perhaps, or maybe twenty-five, forty-plus, ahhh . . . nope. The man will give the women what she wants and this behavior will last until the goal is met. Each side has sufficient reason to be suspect of lies by omission. Many men stop trusting women completely during adolescence. Not distrusting women's behavior, just their motivations. Not distrusting a woman's fidelity or with money or kids, just trusting them completely with their heart. This often occurs at a fairly young age, this can change, bonds can develop, trust can be built but, it is a long process, difficult, and easily disrupted.

Again, the dance will continue and we will still have a struggle finding a relationship that works for us. If the man stays for a relationship, he will continue to show romantic actions to a lesser extent. If he stays for sex, the romance will end almost immediately. This is a good way to know into which sub-group one falls. After that initial marriage/relationship has failed, after we have experienced the grief that comes with the death of that dream we were promised in our youth, we are once again looking and trying to connect and to fall in love again. We are trying to find "The One" once again when the bloom is off the rose and we are older and hopefully wiser. Our relationships are grown up ones and are a matter of attraction, connection, a few absolutes, and sex. The great mystery and desperation of sex that was not well endured in adolescence is gone for men. They have been to the circus, know what it's about and want to find what will make them happy. Men know they have to negotiate less for sex.

Women also have been down that road. They see men more skeptically; no longer as heroes or able to always bring happiness. Often this new freedom allows women to have a better appreciation for intimacy. The ultimate goal is to release all that grief carried for the death of our dream. To look at ourselves and understand our values have little to do with who wants us, that while attraction is part of living and dating, we are subject to how others view us more than we would like. That has always been true and we have just been encouraged to disregard it, which often gives us an excuse for not helping ourselves and provides encouragement to blame others. While not putting in the effort to bring change to ourselves, we get angry at others for not seeing us differently.

To this end, self-reflection is an integral part of who you are and what you want, both as a person and in a relationship. As a woman, if you ask, *"Will you respect me in the morning?"* before sex, you're asking the wrong question. First, ask yourself these questions: *"Do I nag, or tend to be overwhelmed with past relationships? Am I unmarketable, annoying, or tend to be overly emotional?"* If there is a "yes" to any of those questions, the object of your desire will most likely only stay until he is tired of the sex. For men, respect never enters into the equation. For women, respect of oneself is probably the most important key.

Friends First—Analysis

I would like to believe that women really want a friend first, but I don't. I do believe that it is a ploy engaged to attempt to protect the woman and control the interaction between her and a man of her liking. If a woman really believes in "friends first" then she shouldn't have any preferences in who she meets. No serial killers, but as far as height, weight, body shape, or looks there should be no boundaries. If it really is to become friends, there should be none, zero, zip, nada, no concern for the physical or attractiveness aspects of a man. If it is about making a friend and then deciding if a relationship is possible, looks, work, income, etc. shouldn't be in the mix at all. But it isn't, it's not about "friends," it's about meeting a man in that narrow band of "relationship potential" and managing the potential pain and trying to manage the aspects of what the man wants and his selection process. This is a clever maneuver but not really a great plan when considering the outcome as it drives men away and makes them more likely not to want a relationship. It only motivates men who have placed the woman in the Sex Only Sub-Group and they are more likely to lie to achieve the goal. It nearly guarantees a woman will primarily be entertained by those outside the optimum zone. Perhaps this hypocrisy is what makes men so frustrated by the idea of "friends first" when they see it on profiles. It's not an honest phrase and it's seen as misleading. It says loudly to men, "Forget it guys. I have been hurt and you will have to pay for my poor choices." We can agree both men and woman carry extreme imprints of former relationships. Women using "friends first" as a wall and men's reaction can be taken as signs of the pain both carry. It is important for women to understand what men hear and take away from the "friends first" drivel in a profile.

"Friends First" as interpreted by men

- Some guy really hurt you and you're going to take it out on any guy who shows an interest. (that is until you go goofy for one that will hurt you again)

- You don't understand men

- You don't understand male friends

- You don't like sex

- You have been doing sex wrong

- You have been doing sex with the wrong person.

Special note to reader: In a man's way of thinking, if you don't crave sex, nearly all the time you're doing it wrong or with the wrong person—the operative word here being "man's."

The "Friends First" concept also includes no sex on the first date as a philosophical position. It's intended to cause the man to come back for more dates and to get to know the woman and to filter out men who only want sex. While well-intentioned, it does neither and will filter out men who may be good candidates. If men's motivation to date is primarily for sex, even the really "good men"—you know "real men"—who is left to date? Who is left to take a chance on a relationship under such one sided terms? Women express that sex on the first date is often a benchmark of thinking a man will leave, probably because men have left after first date sex. A man's staying or going is not related to sex. Most often that decision was made when he asked the woman out. It won't make a man leave sooner but it may make a man stay longer if it is "rock your world" really great sex. A woman will set boundaries and expectations for some romantic connection and forget the only reason she was asked out was because she was viewed as a potential sex partner. It is only after you get to know someone in person does their uniqueness come through.

If a woman truly wants to avoid one night stands and take control of the sexual aspect of dating, she has to choose sexual partners based upon her needs, not the man's wants. Women have to choose, because they want to be sexual not because the man is applying pressure. Sex has to be what the woman wants to do. Embrace and enjoy it. If the man stays, great; if he leaves, it's okay, too, but the attitude changes the dynamic. Nothing says a woman should ever have sex on the first date or any date for that matter. It is all up to her because this is a personal choice; she just doesn't need to advertise it. As far as the woman is concerned, her actions should depend upon how "Wowed" she is by the man. This takes the focus and pressure off of her and makes it her choice, totally. It does put the pressure onto the man and his presentation. That should be a much better situation for the woman.

The Hurdles

Linier or straight line thinking is when we have a start point and a step by step progression through a process so we can evaluate where we are at each point. These hurdles or benchmarks are set to attempt to keep us on track toward the goal. While valuable for many objective projects, it is a very poor way to make relationship decisions. Women utilize linier thinking in an effort to forestall sexual behavior and to try to ensure a man is committed to them prior to sexual activity. So many dates to third base, commitment before sex, and the like sound like a good process to ensure quality relationships, however emotions tend to take women off the linier track and men tend to escalate pressure and intensity to reach the goal. It all falls apart. The only real issue with this linier thinking is the belief it can be helpful. It is putting feelings and perceptions on hold and placing steps or hurdles in the way to be overcome prior to moving forward. As already discussed a man's decision to stay or go, to have a relationship or not has in most cases been made prior to asking the woman out. Sex won't keep him for much longer if he plans not to stay and sex definitely won't drive him away, unless it's bad sex, if he plans to stay. Lack of sex often will prematurely lead to his departure in either case. It would be nice if there was a "checklist" available which men could follow. Men also have a touch of the linier in their dating process. Often they have a preset amount of dates they will commit to with a woman to achieve their sexual goal. For example, a man may invest three dates on average to determine if the woman is what he wants for a relationship or if she is in the Sex Only group to achieve that goal.

Sex—Part II

We know that woman get to choose about all things sexual. If it's not "yes", it's against the law from holding hands to every level of intercourse imaginable. In our society, it's the women's choice. All the protections are weighted towards the woman regarding choice and sexuality. Understandably this should benefit women in their pursuit of relationships, but it seems to cause anger. I think it is possible that when there is such exclusive control of anything, there is some confusion over the power it generates, how much other's will want it and frustration over someone taking it, or giving it away foolishly. That may be in exchange for what the woman considers as a deserved relationship. This situation seems to produce some anger, and I am not sure if the anger is about men or about having the weight of choice about such a desired object or about having that level of control and screwing it up (read making a poor selection). When you have such power to bestow favor and do it poorly, self-recrimination would likely be the result. The giving of favor to the undeserving becomes brutally painful as a memory. If you hold a thing as a measurement for something else, i.e.

sex only for love, it can only apply if both parties involved have the same perspective. As far as men and women are concerned, that not only isn't true, it isn't possible.

To be clear, for men, having sex or not having sex doesn't change the likelihood of a relationship. If a man is going to leave it matters little if there is sex. Women often are concerned about being thought of as promiscuous. First of all, it should matter more what the woman thinks about herself than what men she doesn't want to be with think of her. Secondly, after the teen years, a woman's sexuality is really only a concern for insecure men or men who have an underlying need to subjugate their partner. The question then becomes, why would an emotionally healthy woman want that kind of man? An emotionally healthy woman would not. Perhaps this would be a good time to ponder that point.

About the same time I learned that good girls don't always sleep alone, I learned to stop measuring a person or judging them based upon adult sexual behavior. This means that judging a person's worth or value on whether they are having sex, or how often, or who with and even questions of monogamy have little to do with love, caring, responsibility, security, success, or support. Sex doesn't affect being a father, a mother, or a career unless it is done in detraction of responsibility, which is wrong—not because of sex but because anything that detracts from being responsible is wrong. It is easy to use sex as a yardstick for good and evil because it's physical, easy to see either/or and black/white. It's an easy line to draw. As we all know, human behavior is never that easy to understand and while motivations may be simple, what causes people to actually choose that course rarely is so simple. Social interactions have become much more complex in terms of sexuality. Humans just haven't changed enough to keep up.

If the man is going to stay, he doesn't care all that much about past sexual behavior. If a man likes a woman, likes the sex, then he will stay. There can be twangs of possessiveness, but if a man likes you he will stay, if not he will go. It is about what the women does for him and what she convinces the man he does for her. That there was sex involved has little to no influence on the outcome.

Jeremiah J. Jordan

The Relationship Sub-Group

Since the book is about relationships we need to look closer at the Relationship Sub-Group. The truly important questions involve how to get into it and stay there. Since the Relationship Sub-Group is so exclusive, even if we start there, it doesn't take much to fall out of contention. Annoying things in profiles or actions can drop us. Men can easily drop from being a potential relationship to the women's "friend zone" quickly and women to the "sex only zone" for men. So, we are back at the beginning. It would be a huge step to never see a woman use "friends first" as their motto. At least they won't run men off. And, use of the phrase does send men packing because it relays so many incorrect messages. Yes, I can hear women saying, *"Well, if they don't like it, they don't deserve me anyway,"* or the popular *"Then I don't want them."* This is saying *"I have all the answers, I am right you are wrong, and if you don't see it my way, I don't want you. And I don't care."* I hope any woman saying this can come to terms with being alone and with their ever revolving door of short term relationships which all end up being painful. Convictions can't keep you warm. As adults we get lonely and we want to be wanted. When women are lonely they want someone to talk to and be reminded that they have value and are special. When men are lonely they want someone to show them they are special and are then willing to talk after . . . well unless they fall asleep. Understanding the differences and the struggles between men and women trying to find adult relationships can be agonizing. The Internet has really helped pass information around . . . and gives us more chances to not be understood or to understand.

It is natural that a woman would want a sense of control over the process. We all want to rule the world, or at least our part of it. The uncertainty of seeking a relationship again after the point in time when they are considered "prime candidates" for male attention can be imposing. But being mature or older doesn't stop people from finding someone. There are many reasons people are alone, most of them because of the person and not for lack of options. Once we are past wanting children, working on careers or struggling to grow up we have more time to consider what we want in a relationship. Men's wants are simple: they like things that catch the eye and that doesn't change with maturity. Women may feel less confident regarding how they look and if they are uncomfortable it will show through. Oddly, in personal ads, women who know they are attractive will express greater range of access, likely because they know they have the control and they will be weeding out applicants instead of hoping for one. A prior marriage tells us what we don't want. We learn a great deal about poor choices and swear we will never do that again, yet seem to return to the same behaviors that got us here.

Moving On

I believe I had an experience when I was young that was experienced by most of my peers. I was heartbroken by someone I trusted. I truly didn't know the depth of despair that we could endure until that happened. Realistically, many other things in my life have been more devastating but that took years of perspective and wisdom to realize. As far as emotional impact, it was a monumental loss. It also was a loss which was preventable, and in retrospect should have been anticipated and predicted and I should have entered into the situation with a much more cavalier attitude than going in with visions of "The One." A nice girl, yes, beautiful yes, but "The One"—not even close. Of course, I am seeing it through my much older eyes. Yes, I moved on, I did get over it, and trudged onto more of life. Yes, I carried with me, for many years, the lessons learned from that and never really forgave myself for allowing myself to be hurt that way. I kept the hope for "The One" after that error in judgment for quite a while. It then came to me. At the beginning of a relationship, someone can truly appear to be "The One." Only during the part when we are being emotionally disemboweled do we realize we made an error and that is a poor time to do character building. After making several more runs at relationship bliss, and enduring the death of The Dream, time began to mold thoughts, desires and expectations. Realizing I no longer was looking for "The One," I took some time to figure out what I was looking for. Understanding that I would never be the naïve boy and young man of years gone by, did I have to accept being jaded and cynical about the process of dating and of women in general. Many of my male friends were quite past being reasonable as they spoke almost contemptuously of women. Yes, we would have been much better off to have found "The One" and spent our lives with them. I am not going to rehash the idea of a forever relationship or divorce or all the nostalgic concepts which have no bearing on the here and now. The reality to me and many of us is that what we once thought to be the way is no longer available. While our grieving for the lost dream is real, the idea that "The One" exists will very much interfere with our ability to find someone with whom we can love and share happiness. The most realistic answer for people who are looking for "The One" would be, after forty years, if they aren't with you . . . you either discarded them, drove them away, or they took a look at you and they aren't coming.

Age is a wonderful thing for relationships if you can put down the old baggage and enjoy. If one expects "The One" to suddenly walk into your life, you likely will be eternally disappointed. If you stop throwing rocks, stop trying to change others, work on improving yourself, a "one-like" person may come along. For a woman, the most critical aspect of being able to successfully date, develop a connected relationship and enjoy it, is to accept men as they are. That doesn't mean you shouldn't expect to be treated well—you should actually demand better treatment, better manners, and thoughtfulness. Say things to encourage an intellectual dialogue. If he can't converse in a satisfactory way, you know he may not be for you. Ask meaningful questions. A good sign of how a man perceives the world can be gained by a few simple answers and some observations.

- o   Does he eat with a hat on?

- o   Does he put his cart in the cart corral or leave it for someone else?

- o   Does he talk to his mother as a servant?

- o   Does he understand what contrition means and can he demonstrate it?

- o   Does he serve his kids needs or do they serve his?

- o   Does he know when to be quiet?

- o   Does he realize your mood changed and how did he respond?

o   Does his mood change for no apparent reason?

There are no correct answers, since it's your choice of who you spend time with and we can't help who we love. Whatever the answers may be, it gives you a clearer picture of the man you are with. And if there are two or more answers that don't mesh with your expectations, run, don't walk, run away. The reason you're searching now is because you didn't do a very good job the first time.

I won't settle . . . !

A common thread we hear from women is that they won't settle. Actually it's more like they won't settle again. For some they won't settle for the third or fourth time. It must be true because it's pasted into thousands of women's profiles. There are things you don't need to settle for, though. Things like abuse, prior incarceration or outstanding warrants for arrest, significant debt, or unresolved prior relationship issues are at the top of a very short list. All of these are pretty easy to see because men quickly will relax and their nature will come out if you will just take a look. Men are simple. Just watch, listen, and make sure he sees the world in a way you can appreciate and not just put up with because you already know you can't put up with it.

So it's up to you to decide. The Group Wilson-Phillips on their album of the same name had a hit song that so well spoke to the situation of being an adult trying again to find happiness. The lyrics pose a haunting question which goes to the heart of moving on:

You can sustain or are you comfortable with the pain?

You've got no one to blame for your unhappiness

You got yourself into you own mess.

—Chynna Phillips, Carnie Wilson and Glen Ballard

As children and teens we were subject to what we were told and an abundance of overwhelming emotions which made everything feel more intense. The impact of the loss of our dream follows us. Often our children came from that failed relationship, an ever present reminder of our past error in judgment. Not the children themselves, but they are a reminder and we can't get over it, sometimes because the roots of the failure we still carry with us. If we are delusional enough we can even say that it was all our former partner's fault. We can come up with many reasons for its failure which often take us away from why it did. Perhaps it was the wrong person to begin with. Perhaps we should have known better. Perhaps we just lost them and now we want to find someone as wonderful as they were. No matter how The Dream died, have the funeral, gather your friends, and say goodbye.

The most important aspect of finding someone with whom you can be happy is putting yourself into a place mentally, physically and emotionally to be able to date and have a relationship. If you are angry you're not ready. If you are distrusting of men, you're not ready. If you feel you need to get in shape, lose forty pounds or color your hair before you can be acceptable to someone you believe will make you happy, you're not ready. We have all heard this over and over and it rings true, we just ignore it. If we don't like ourselves, no one else can like us. I don't use the word love because people can love us when we hate ourselves. We must not confuse that, but if you are not what you feel you should be it will come through in dating. That doesn't mean you have to be anything more than the best you can be. All of us are loveable if we put the hate and anger and pain where it belongs, back in the relationship we got it from through forgiveness and resolution, and not into the one we are trying to begin.

Real Men, Good Men and Going Slow

"I want a *real* man." Women often make this statement. This statement is often made with an angry undertone in an attempt to berate or guilt men into certain behaviors. It's very confusing to men because there is no clear definition of a "real man." Also, any definition a woman has is miles away from what any man would consider accurate. Again, we are on opposite sides and women don't seem to understand that it drives potentially good men away. It is truly surprising a woman would use it and show how little she knows about men and how little she cares what they think or feel. Men believe a "real man" to a woman must be Prince Charming/Storybook hero-calm level headed, faithful, interested, never looks elsewhere and does what he is told (probably likes to go shopping). In film or TV, men in romantic comedies; romantic, heart on sleeve, vulnerable, cares totally about the woman, even when wrong. The man's inner self is open and emotive. Loves pets, children, and likes long walks talking about nothing . . . works to live not lives to work (and does what he is told). Get all their reinforcement from family and woman not work, or accomplishment. Makes tons of money but never is at work. Oh yes, and is good for the environment. I have looked; I don't know any men like that.

To men, a "real" man is James Bond—love 'em and leave 'em, a man who attracts almost *any* woman and never becomes emotionally attached. It's all about sex and when there are emotions, duty comes first. Children, pets, family and friends are things he can't afford to care about because of duty, commitment to it, and his buddies. He fights, is responsible, committed to work. Relationships get in the way of being a man. There is a big difference between the sexes' ideas of what a "real man" is and is about.

So why do women continue to insult men by saying they're looking for a "real man" by their own definition? Do they really think they will guilt them into liking them because of it, or will it make the man be like they want them to be? For men, being a real man has nothing to do with relationships. All it tells men is that the woman has been hurt and is angry and likely more difficult to deal with. A woman's cost for this comment is two attraction points which immediately drops her out of the Relationship Sub-Group.

A Good Man. This is again a large difference in concepts between men and women. "A good man" seems to be another term that can be used to instill guilt in men but often backfires. To men, a good man doesn't speak to relationships so much as to fairness and hard work. President Clinton is considered a good man, although not monogamous by any stretch of the imagination. Dennis Rader, (known as the BTK Killer), was not a good man but by all accounts, was a church goer, faithful husband, and caring father. The idea of being a "Good Man" has more to do with acts toward the world and not acts connected to a relationship. Right or wrong, they build statues to men who achieve success or glory but destroy their family, philandering and playing while a quiet, faithful, caring man who provides for and is good to his family is considered a career failure. Perhaps women should have a meeting and decide what is important and what terms to use in describing men. It won't change men but might help women stop shooting themselves in the foot trying to find a relationship.

"Going Slow" seems another way of saying "no sex" or "friends first," because a man reads the same things into it. With emotions there is no fast or slow, you either do or don't; perhaps that is why men tend to be so quickly invested if the female is in the Relationship Sub-Zone. Men jump in quickly in and try to make it work, until their effort fails, then they are as quickly disinvested. For men, because of how they select, there is no slow. It takes about 12 seconds to make the decision. Men will agree with "going slow," acts to support "going slow," but will always look for opportunities to speed things up.

Marketing 101

Women often try to make a point with statements which seem to be intended to guilt a man into a certain behavior. Notions a woman has about herself and how she is received often come through inadvertently, which can be taken by men much differently than intended. Saying things like *"If you're looking for a Barbie, or a model,"* offend men and tell them you are angry and probably physically unattractive. Stop saying it. Leave it to the guy to determine you're attractiveness. Stop saying BBW in your profile. If you're attractive say that, if your large say that; let the man determine if he is attracted to you without putting yourself into a box. Men have done pretty well over the years and will be able to tell if they are interested in you . . . or not.

If you are happy with yourself as a person, you won't have to warn men what to expect, by trying to guilt or categorize them. If you aren't happy with yourself and apologize for it, it only frustrates men and causes them to alter the search so that the only men you will likely attract are those wanting only just sex and not a relationship. If you say "Friends First" or "no sex," you have removed all motivation from the man to go out with you . . . period. Even if they still want to go out with you because of attraction, it will likely drop you out of the Relationship Sub-Group because, again, *men want sex.* That doesn't mean they have to get it, but stop saying they won't. Men know the decision is all up to you. Men also know from those types of statements they already have a hill to climb with your existing issues about males. Don't add more. Stop saying things like *"My friends tell me I have a great personality, am outgoing and caring."* What are you friends supposed to say? Men don't ask women out for those reasons. These are all good point and necessary for a relationship but not for a date.

Some clarity about media and advertising artificially driving desire is needed. Is it possible that a group in a room somewhere selects what the rest of us will find desirable and attractive? For instance, women/political/social groups express the idea that there is a certain type of feminine form that is considered ideal or most desirable because the media puts it in front of us and guides our tastes. While fashion has changed throughout the years, desire hasn't. We like what we like. If we didn't, those paying for the advertising would show us something else. That being said, the appreciation of the feminine form has remained pretty constant since mankind began drawing on cave walls. I would generally say what man found attractive 10,000 years ago he finds attractive today as well. Perhaps instead of trying to guilt men into wanting something they don't want, an easier route is becoming something they want. Of course, that would be giving in and it is always much more productive to be angry and throw rocks at passersby hoping one of them will understand your in pain and love you.

Ending

I heard a great motto for people to live by. *If you want to be happy, lower your expectations.* The converse of that is raising your level of existence. Being human as we are, it's too much work to elevate ourselves and we are too stubborn to lower our expectations, so it is easier to do neither and gripe about it. Welcome to the human condition. There are times we all would trade everything we have for someone to care about us. Then there are times when someone does, and it's not enough because it's not the right person. We all want what we want when we want it. We throw away opportunity because it doesn't fit our concept of "The One." Women often express that they want to find or are searching for their soul mate. This seems to be combined with a long litany of things men have done wrong to them. This is pointing to "The One" belief system which, we should understand as grown-ups, doesn't work and is counterproductive to any effort to find happiness. You may find a one-like person or them you, however all that "not settling" dialogue and advertising only chases them away before you meet them. I always enjoy the cute saying, "looking for Mr. Right, not Mr. Right Now." As clever as the idiom is, it tells men you are carrying a very large amount of emotional baggage from past relationships. Additionally, you had your chance to pick Mr. Right at least once and more likely several times. What makes you think you will be any better choosing this time? Perhaps you are or perhaps you aren't, but there's no need in driving a potential Mr. Really Good Options away. Again, the choice is yours. Do you wish to be alone, or do you wish to consider a different perspective? I don't think either men or women can change who they are or change their nature. However, since the nature of men is primarily instinctive and a woman's nature is more emotional, perhaps what is behind door number three may work better. A bit of intellect to be used on both sides may help make some progress.

Men, as far as why they date, how they select who they date and their groupings will not change. It hasn't for 25,000 years and men have little motivation to force a change. Let me say that a little more clearly MEN WON'T CHANGE. Men will continue to ask out only women with whom they want to have sex. Men won't tell if the women is or isn't in the Relationship Sub-Group. Men absolutely will act as if they are in hopes of garnering favor and therefore sex. Sex neither causes the man to leave or to stay and will have little to no effect on that choice. Understand that this is life.

That doesn't mean a woman can't get what she wants and in a manner she wants. Understand it, adapt, use it, enjoy it, and have a chance of being happier.

A Change in Strategy

I don't believe women will make the huge jump in methods so as to risk the rejection of asking out men with whom they wish to get to know. Several factors influence that; however, the greatest is fear of being rejected. It is easy to ask a man to be sexual; it is much harder to ask *"Do want to spend time with me under my terms with no sex involved?"* You would see a lot of men squirm trying to find an answer. It would also be painful to women since they are not being irrationally driven by testosterone to overcome rejection and try again. Women, especially when adolescents, take being not enough as massively defeating as do boys with similar deep scars. Fortunately, boys grow up and become thoughtless men. How else could they ever approach a woman again? A further complication with a woman making the overture to date occurs because a man only asks a woman he views as a potential sex partner. At that point, the man is ready to have sex. Well, he wants to have sex. Many men won't be able to understand why the woman doesn't want to have sex right way and skip dinner. Neither men nor women are the problem in this scenario. It's just that both are seeing the other as they see themselves, not accounting for the significant difference in perspective. So, if women are unlikely to change that part of the equation, what can they do to make dating more possible?

Remember that men are not good at subtle clues about interest. Most of them cannot tell the difference between flirtation and being nice. Men also know whichever one they choose, it will be the other one. So, if a man is nice to you, and you want to know more, let him know. Don't ask him on a date; just let him know it is flirting and not just being nice. If a woman hands a man her phone number in a bar, he will think it means the woman wants sex. Men are programmed to think that. The woman may or may not but that can be cleared up if he calls. Men ask for numbers knowing often it's a fake number or they are in competition to see how many numbers they can get. It's considerably more significant if a woman gives the man her phone number or email address. Again, we must remember the woman is in control of what happens. Women can market pretty aggressively to expand their options, and since it's in their control what happens, that isn't a bad idea. Men's dating options are much larger due to their motivation to date; women have similar groupings but seek more from whom they date. A simple fact of sales: you have to be in front of the customer before you can make a sale. You have to get in front of the man for any chance of a relationship. The other side of that situation is you also have to see if you actually like the guy.

The 1% Rule

Take for instance the predominantly male outlook on internet dating. It is a shotgun approach. The goal of the approach is to contact every woman that appears in his YES group. Generally, Sub-Group A is exempt from the shotgun approach, but then again it never hurts to be thorough. This again illustrates the numbers mentality. While not knowing the exact numbers, to a man, if they are to connect with one percent of the female population as a potential relationship partner, then they need to see a thousand so they can at least have options. Somewhat like a needle in a haystack approach, if we proactively approach dating, rather than having faith in the accidental connection with "The One," we can provide ourselves with the most positive possible outcome. So if the man contacts one-hundred females and if ten reply and five are sorted out and conversation begins with two and the man meets one, those aren't bad odds.

Sex Talk

Sexual conversation while getting to know each other is often thought of by the woman as an indication of the man's only interest. She would be mistaken. If a man goes out or asks a woman out on a date, he probably desires sex with her. It is on his mind anyway or else he wouldn't be there. The man is attempting to get some idea from the women about her feelings about sexuality, and if they are close to a match expectation wise. He is also trying to implant the thought of being sexual with him so as to get her used to the idea. Not a real smooth move but, since he is thinking about being sexual, it comes out and sometimes clumsily. An honest upfront man will talk about sex, because if he is attracted to a woman he is thinking about it. If he asked you out, he is attracted to you. If a man doesn't talk about sex, it is because he is: 1) cautious, or 2) quiet or 3) not as direct (read lying). To either 1 or 2, if you're in the Relationship Zone, it's not all about sex. If you are not in that sub-group, then it is totally about sex, no matter what! How is a woman supposed to know? Well, until you have sex you don't really have a way of finding out. If they leave, you don't really know, other than knowing you were not in their Relationship Sub-Group.

What is important about the discussion is that the two of you are on the same sexual page. If not, it's as important to know as if you are. That doesn't mean anything has to come of the conversation. The woman is in control. There is plenty of time for "no" whenever it needs to come into play. Along with those sexual conversations, never tell a man what you have done with another man that you won't do with him. This is a zero win circumstance as it creates a competition between the man and your ex. It immediately makes him feel you loved someone else more than him. I never said men made sense, just that they are simple. If you have done anything you are positive you don't want to do again, explain it as a medical condition, trauma, or female issue. For most men, we will nod and say "okay." This works very well if you follow the explanation by touching his arm and saying with a smile, *"Were it not for that, I would love for us to."*

Rock Throwing

For some reason, both sexes seem to have to throw rocks at the other gender. Unfortunately, we don't always throw those rocks at the right portion of the other gender. In military terms, it's called collateral damage—the unfortunate damage we do to bystanders when we throw big rocks, or in the case of the military, drop bombs. We throw huge communication rocks and then have to suffer for the consequence of our poor planning. For women this relates to several things discussed earlier about communication. There are vast differences and misperceptions that both men and women have about what they say and how what they say is perceived. Men's behavior is very consistent so it makes sense to utilize that knowledge to a woman's advantage. To do that, and open up the most options available, a few small communication issues must be tweaked. Okay, tweaked is not the correct word for what needs occur. To be clearer, women have to totally stop—completely, without exception—some communication behaviors. Do I believe that this will happen? No! Nor will those pigs I spoke of in Chapter 5 ever fly.

But if it were to occur, any woman who did make the adjustment would see a huge difference in how she was perceived, the amount of communication she received, and the tone of that communication. First of all, as was earlier discussed, stop bashing men with stupid, moronic statements that can only alienate men from possibly wanting anything but sex and to run away as fast as possible afterward. Secondly, most importantly, and directly relating to the whole purpose of this book: never say "Friends First" again. Even if in your heart you mean it with every fiber of your being. Don't utter those words. No matter how you explain it, no matter your intention, no matter that you can't sit still wanting to start your communication with that thought, remember that when you use it, men—even the best of them—hate the word, and downgrade you to Sub-Group C due to suspected damage. By using "Friends First" and male bashing you almost always guarantee that the only men who will ask you out are those who put you in Sub Group C and will go out only as long as it takes to get sex. Your effort to protect yourself misguidedly brings wolves to the door, starting the cycle again.

With a slight change in presentation and perspective I believe:

- o you can have a more healthy relationship
- o you can avoid one night stands
- o you can love, be loved, and not be alone

To get these you have to accept some aspects of men and life:

- o you cannot find "The One" (he doesn't exist),
- o Prince Charming, Soul Mate and Mr. Right (beyond right now) are not doing online dating.
- o you cannot expect men to change
- o you cannot expect men to feel as you do

Most men want a relationship badly, more than they will admit. As stated before they just want sex on their way to finding it. For men it's a part of the journey. We have established that in dating, women get to choose, pretty much about everything and hopefully they make good choices. For women to have a chance at happiness, choices must be based upon want and need without hoping it will keep the man from leaving or make him happy enough to stay. A tough lesson to learn but that change in perspective will make drastic changes in outcomes and feelings of self-worth.

A man's perspective of what constitutes having a good time is different than a woman's. This shouldn't be a surprise and again this isn't bad, it just is. A man has much more fun being out with his guy friends and that will often trump hanging with the girlfriend (significant other, wife, etc.). He will hang out with a woman, go where she wants to go and, once children are involved, responsible men will be just that—responsible. Again, as far as having a good time, hanging with the guys is impossible to beat. You don't have to behave, watch what you say, not insult anyone, not be politically correct, look at women and talk about what it would be like *if*. The lesson here is accept it, and don't try to beat it or beat it out of him. Knowing he is with you because you want him to be is what matters to him and should to you. All the things men do, romantic, helping at home, "special occasion" cards, your favorite place to eat, they do from choice. Not because anything in their emotional make up prompts them. They are thinking of you by choice. This is a very, very good thing and one that should be cherished not admonished. Men will never want to do many things, but they will do them smiling because the woman wants to. That is a significant piece of behavior to appreciate, and perhaps if it was rewarded more often, you wouldn't be reading this book.

In the fast paced, complex world of today, it can be easy for a woman to forget that men are simple. Once attraction is satisfied, they want to like the woman and to enjoy spending time with her. Men wish to not be driven crazy, nor to be reminded of their ex-wife. Men want a woman who doesn't nag, or try to change them. As seen over and over, when a women does try to make her man change, he will resist and resent her for the effort. He then will resent the person and then the woman is back where she started, alone.

Men and women have fought and coupled for thousands of years. We can be pretty sure neither the fighting nor the problems with coupling will change much in the future. Men and women have struggled with how to make relationships work for just as long. Nothing in this book will change the things which bring men and women into conflict when dating. Those things are far to ingrained into us. What may change perhaps is that women, the really brave ones, may decide to drop the failed methodology and give something new a shot. They may see the benefit in acceptance and utilizing knowledge to help them find a partner who will love them and they can love. If only one brave, beautiful, loving woman makes that happen, then I have succeeded in what I have set out to do.

CPSIA information can be obtained at www.ICGtesting.com
Printed in the USA
BVOW070129220312

285735BV00001B/54/P